WILD swimming Alps

130 most beautiful lakes, rivers & waterfalls in Austria, Germany, Switzerland, Italy & Slovenia.

Hansjörg Ransmayr

WILD THINGS PUBLISHING

WILD swimming
Alps

130 most beautiful
lakes, rivers & waterfalls in
Austria, Germany, Switzerland,
Italy & Slovenia.

Hansjörg Ransmayr

WILD
THINGS
PUBLISHING

Rio Salto, Maggia (93)

CONTENTS

MAP OF SWIMS

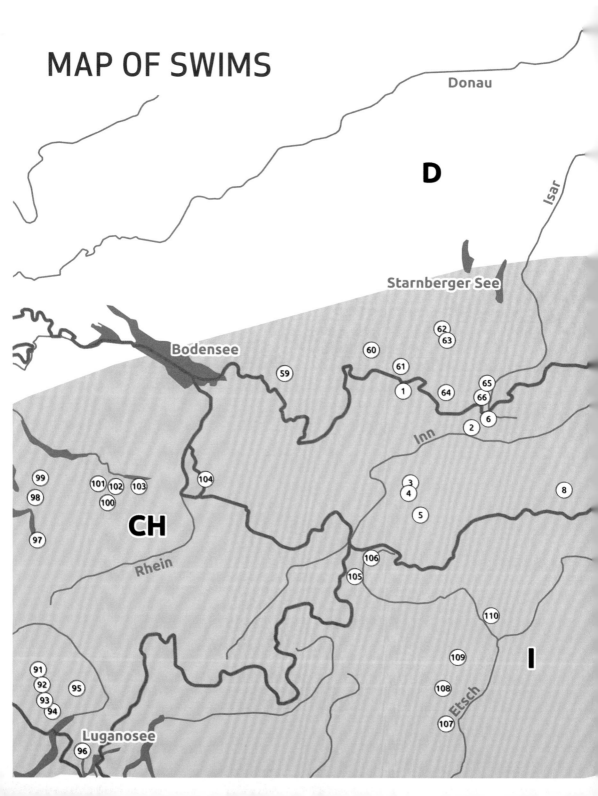

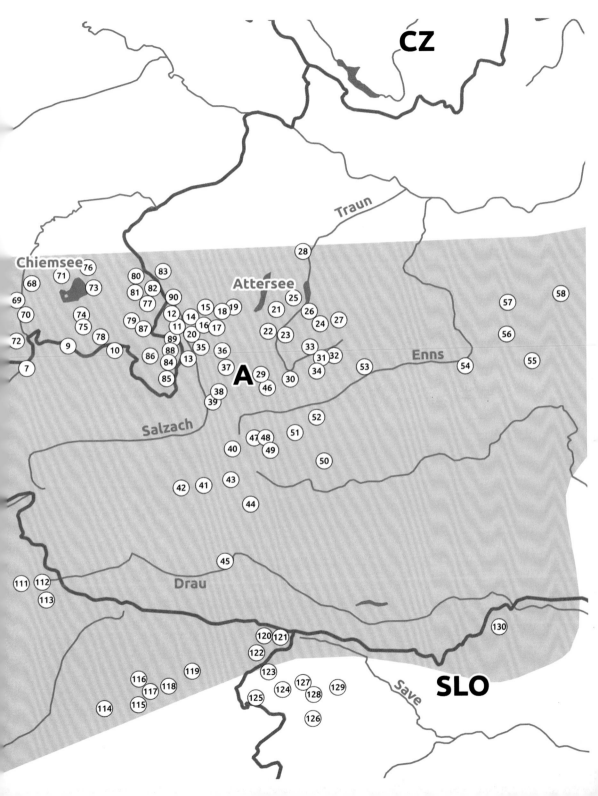

GIVE ME FIVE...

The pilgrimage church of St Bartholomä on
the western shore of Lake Königssee (85a)

THE FIVE BEST PLACES TO EAT BY WATER

THE FIVE MOST ACCESSIBLE SPOTS

THE FIVE MOST FAMILY-FRIENDLY SPOTS

THE FIVE MOST CHALLENGING SPOTS

RESPECT & RESPONSIBILITY

The river Salza, Wildalpen (56)

SENSITIVE HABITATS

Of course, it would be great to just jump into the clear water straight away, but it is really important to choose the right entry point. At spots that attract many bathers, the suitable entry points are already laid out for all to see, so that you only need to use your common sense.

There is, however, one definite no-no: never make your way to the water by ploughing through reed beds, water lilies or marshy areas, because these are nesting and spawning areas around lakes and rivers and must not be disturbed. If you cannot find a reasonable way to access the water, please move on to the next swimming spot.

This also applies to shallow pools and ponds with poor drainage, especially in a hot summer or after prolonged periods with little rainfall. This is because these bodies of water are particularly sensitive to disturbance and easily damaged by swimmers.

RESPECT OTHER PEOPLE

Wild swimming is for people who love freedom, and this is pretty obvious. However, it can sometimes be easy to forget that your freedom crosses a line when it begins to impair the freedom of others. In general, wild swimmers are very aware of respecting other people. That doesn't mean that there have to be restrictions everywhere. For example, those who like to listen to music can put their headphones on, and, if you want to play with your dog by the bathing spot, just make sure that you don't disturb other people. If you can see a fisherman's line in the water ahead of you, please move on to another nearby swimming spot. This way, everyone can enjoy nature doing what they love. One last point, if I may: please only camp and make a fire in designated areas.

LEAVE NO TRACE

"Do not leave anything behind apart from the ripples that radiate from your body while swimming." Isn't this a beautiful credo? Putting this principle into action is not as difficult as it might sound, although in reality things can be a little more complicated. Even if I run the risk of repeating myself, please do not leave anything behind in these wonderful bathing spots: no picnic leftovers, no cigarette stumps, no beer cans, nothing at all!

One should always leave a bathing or swimming spot in as clean a state as one found it – or even cleaner. Thank you for being respectful!

SAFETY FIRST

Buchenegg waterfalls (56)

AVOID COLLISIONS

Diving off cliffs, bridges, swinging ropes or rope swings can be great fun and give you a real kick. However, accidents do happen and it is best to observe a few rules to avoid injuries.

First of all, don't jump into anything before you have checked what is below the surface. Often, pools that are deep in certain places also contain rocks that significantly reduce the depth of the water.

Also, these kinds of checks should be carried out right before you are going to dive, because local conditions can change suddenly and what was perfectly safe last time you visited can be hazardous today. It is possible that the current or high waters have deposited roots-rocks, sharp branches, sandbanks or even rocks in the meantime. It should go without saying that you shouldn't bathe or swim after thunderstorms or at high water when rivers and streams can carry bits of trees and other large material. And there should particularly be no swimming below cascades or waterfalls in these conditions!

THE DECEPTIVE POWER OF WATER

Naturally, you want to jump into the water straight away, but this can easily backfire.

For running water, it is essential to choose the right entry and exit points. It will often not be possible to enter and exit the water in the same place. Always bear in mind that the riverbank downstream might be steep, thorny or slippery.

Downstream from man-made constructions, such as weirs or current-slowing facilities in particular, a dangerous pull can develop that doesn't allow swimmers to escape from the water. Many of these hazardous spots can appear entirely harmless from the riverbank. If in doubt, do not enter the water in these locations and keep a sufficiently safe distance.

Downstream of power stations, reservoirs and the like you should always be aware that the water table might rise extremely quickly. The narrower or steeper a river section, the more powerful and dangerous these sudden bursts of water can be. In whitewater, loosely stacked boulders are the greatest hazard. This is because, while the water can flow through and underneath such rocks, a swimmer who is dragged by the current may not necessarily be so fortunate. Also, please note that in wild streams with a strong current you should always swim downstream with your legs pointing forward.

THOSE WHO LOVE HOT SHOWERS, TAKE CARE!

The infamous prison island of Alcatraz in the Bay of San Francisco was one institution where the inmates were forced to take hot showers. The reason behind this strange rule was to avoid the prisoners being given a chance to get used to the ice-cold waters in the ocean around the island, which meant that there was virtually no way of escaping from Alcatraz. Therefore, if you love a hot shower and are used to it, please approach cold open water with caution. The best and most natural way to get accustomed to cold water is to keep swimming from summer right into the winter season. In this way, your body can gradually get used to the dropping temperatures. Even if you are an experienced swimmer, you should never underestimate the effect that cold water temperatures can have on your swimming. Swimming 500m in a heated pool is completely different to swimming 500m in a cold mountain tarn! If you are planning to swim long distances in cold or unknown bodies of water, or those with heavy shipping traffic, you should always take a swim buoy with you.

IS IT CLEAN?

Naturally, the swimming spots recommended to you in this guide generally have excellent water quality. However, nature can be moody and, after heavy rainfall or floods, the water might be temporarily polluted, making safe bathing impossible. In most cases, this is due to drainage systems becoming overloaded. As a result, the water quality is impaired by road dirt; industrial, urban and agricultural waste; and leakage from septic tanks. Obviously, dead fish on the banks or in water are never a good sign, and you are well-advised to avoid bathing there. By the way, there is one thing you can do to actively contribute to the water quality: abstain from using sun protection products.

BEWARE OF THUNDERSTORMS

If you are out and about in the Alps, it is always good to keep an eye on the weather, which can change very quickly in the mountains. This is even more important if you are close to or in bodies of water. A thunderstorm in the upper reaches of a river can make it swell in a flash or make the terrain impassable.

Swimmers in a thunderstorm are at maximum risk of injury from lightning. Don't wait until the thunderstorm is almost overhead: leave the water in good time!

NO FLIP-FLOPS PLEASE

Flip-flops aren't any suitable footwear for wild swimmers. The more alpine the environment in which you are moving, the more important it is to choose the right shoes. For long, dry ascents, hiking shoes or mountaineering boots are recommended, whereas hikes through wet canyons require canyoning shoes. To protect your feet, it is best to wear beach shoes or neoprene shoes when entering the water, because you never know what lies below.

KEEP A CLOSE EYE ON THE CHILDREN – AND YOUR ALCOHOL INTAKE!

Please excuse me for going on about this, but it cannot be said often enough that children must never be left unsupervised when close to the water. This applies to wild swimming spots, in particular. Even if you think you have protected your children sufficiently by making them wear inflatable armbands, water wings, floaties or life jackets, none of these items are a substitute for keeping a close eye on them.

And to be good supervisors, parents need a clear head, which leads us to the next topic. Statistics show that in about 70 per cent of all bathing accidents, alcohol is involved. Therefore, please be aware of the units and stay safe to have more fun!

(52a) Hüttensee

AUSTRIA

A DECLARATION OF LOVE TO A SMALL BUT FANTASTIC COUNTRY

The "alpine republic" of Austria offers wild swimming fans a huge range of possibilities – from idyllic forest and meadow lakes in the flatter foothills of the Alps to picturesque river bathing spots in the uplands and alpine swimming adventures. Arguably the most spectacular spot could be the backdrop to a James Bond movie: It is located in an ice palace under the "perpetual ice" of the Central Alps. The extensive region of the Ötztal Alps has many fabulous mountain lakes and tarns, some of which are at altitudes and in locations that are difficult to access. In comparison to the Ötztal valley, the Pitztal valley, which runs parallel, is far less developed and less frequented by tourists.

01

Stuibenfälle, Reutte

AMMERGAU
ALPS

From the car park behind the Plansee power station, follow the signs to "Stuibenfälle". The secured trail leads past small waterfalls and pools to the big Stuiben fall with its lovely natural pool. Whereas the hike is easy, the descent to the bathing spots can be tricky in places. If you prefer uncomplicated bathing fun and longer swimming stretches, you might be better off at the nearby lakes Plansee or Urisee.

→ **Directions:**
Approaching from the north, exit the A95 at Oberau and continue in the direction of Garmisch-Partenkirchen. From Ehrwald, Lermoos, take Route B179 towards Reutte. If you are coming from the south, exit the A12 at Imst and continue via the Fern Pass.

→ **GPS:** 47.48903, 10.73796

02

PADDLING CLOSE TO THE BORDER –
Möserer See, Seefeld

This calm marsh lake is located in the Olympic region of Seefeld at approx. 1,295m. In summer, it can warm to 25°C and is popular with local people for bathing. The lake is part of a nature reserve with fascinating flora and fauna, a variety of hiking trails and a cosy lakeside pub.

→ **Directions:**
Take Route B177 to Seefeld and then follow Route Möserer Landesstraße to the village of Alt Mösern and the forest car park above Hotel Tyrol.

→ **GPS:** 47.31563, 11.14383

03

ÖTZTAL ALPS

PURE ROMANTICISM –
Lake Brechsee,
St Leonhard im Pitztal

From the car park at the Felsenhof inn, it is a
45-minute walk to the Mauchelalm, which has
catering facilities. The hike continues through
magnificent mountain forest for another hour
to this jewel of a lake in an idyllic alpine valley
at 2,145m.

→ **Directions:**
   Exit the A12 at Imst and follow the Pitztaler Landesstraße (Route L16) into the valley. After St
   Leonhard, turn right to the hamlet of Zaunhof and continue in the direction of Rehwald until you
   get to the Felsenhof inn.

→ **GPS:** 47.09418, 10.79214

04
ÖTZTAL ALPS

SMALL POOL, GREAT SCENERY –
Lake Krummer See,
St Leonhard im Pitztal

For those who love to swim in high alpine lakes and are not put off by low water temperatures, Lake Krummer See is highly recommended. It is one level higher than Lake Brechsee (3), by approx. 300m, and requires an additional ascent of 90 minutes. During the hike, and if you are lucky, you may be able to spot a herd of chamois.

→ **Directions:**
For directions and for the ascent, see spot 3.

→ **GPS:** 47.08574, 10.78132

05
ÖTZTAL ALPS

IDEAL FOR A QUICK DIP OR FOR CANYONING –
Rifflsee, Mandarfen

You can get to this lake at an altitude of 2,300m with the Rifflsee cable car, which has comfortable cabins for six people. The lake's water is rather opaque due to the glacier runoff, but the mountain panorama is truly impressive. Lake Rifflsee doesn't just offer bathing fun and the highest rafting trip in Europe; you can also use it as a starting point for the approx. 2-hour hike to Lake Plodersee at 2,475m.

→ **Directions:**
For directions, see spot 3. Continue on Route L16 to Mandarfen.

→ **GPS:** 46.96535, 10.84876

Upper Isar, Scharnitz

The road is closed for private cars soon after Scharnitz. Depending on the water level and your thirst for adventure, you can find bathing spots in the breathtakingly fresh mountain water closer to Scharnitz (a) or upstream in the narrower, rockier terrain. Also, you don't want to miss out on a "whirlpool bath" in the gorge of the neighbouring Gleirschbach stream (b) at one of the numerous waterfall cascades.

→ **Directions:**
Coming from the north or south, take Route E533 to Scharnitz and park at the end of the village, direction Isar valley. From here, continue on a mountain bike or by "paddle taxi".

→ **GPS:** (a), (b) 47.39199, 11.26517

PERFECT FOR FUN AND GAMES IN THE WATER –
Längsee, Kufstein

Lake Längsee is hidden in the forest and is the least accessible of the four Thierberg lakes in the "Kufsteinerland" (the region around Kufstein). Its shores are steep and there are few sunbathing spots, which is why the lake is not particularly attractive to bathers. On the other hand, its inaccessibility means that Lake Längsee has preserved its wildness. True pathfinders will surely find ways to get down to the water where they will be rewarded with pleasant water temperatures and an experience of unspoilt nature.

→ **Directions:**
Exit the A12 at Kufstein and take Route B171 and Thiersee Landesstraße to the lake.

→ **GPS:** 47.60106, 12.15691

POPULAR FOR ITS DIVING EVENT –

Ice Lake in Nature's Ice Palace, Hintertux

If you are looking for the ultimate wild-swimming challenge in the Alps, here it is: the ice lake of Nature's Ice Palace! It is in the belly of the Hintertux glacier, and it is awesome: an 80m-long ice pool with a 30m-deep, water-filled shaft in its centre, with water and air temperatures that are just above freezing, at an altitude of 3,200m. Are you up for this adventure in the glacier's skiing region? If so, please visit alpineswimming.com or send an email to h.ransmayr@me.com.

→ **Directions:**
Exit the A12 at Zillertal and take Route B169 into the valley to Gstan. Turn right and follow the bendy Tuxer Landesstraße route to the car park by the cable car at the end of the valley.

→ **GPS:** 47.06618, 11.67948

09

ALMOST TOO BEAUTIFUL –
Entenlochklamm, Kössen

In the border region of Tyrol and Bavaria, between Kössen and Ettenhausen, the river Großache makes its way northbound through the mountains. At the pilgrimage village of Maria Klobenstein, where you can find a good swimming spot below the bridge, the river changes its name to Tiroler Ache. Along its course, the river offers several beautiful spots for wild bathing and swimming before, 30km further north, it flows through a protected delta into the big Lake Chiemsee.

→ **Directions:**
Coming from the north, exit the motorway Munich–Salzburg at Grassau and follow Route B305/307 via Schleching to Maria Klobenstein. When approaching from the south, take Route B176 from St Johann in Tirol.

→ **GPS:** 47.68919, 12.39589

10

CHIEMGAU
ALPS

A GRANDIOSE SPECTACLE OF NATURE –
Fischbach, Unken

The Heutal valley is the starting point for a wonderful gorge hike that features two impressive waterfalls and countless picturesque bathing spots. You can park the car (for a fee) at the Heutal lifts. From there, follow the signs to Staubfall. After an approx. 10-minute walk, you reach the imposing Fischbach waterfall and pools, accessed via a steep beaten track downhill.

→ **Directions:**
The village of Unken is on Route B21 through the district of Berchtesgadener Land between the city of Salzburg and Lofer im Pinzgau. When entering the village of Unken, follow the signs to "Heutal-Lifte".

→ **GPS:** 47.66548, 12.65179

The outlet of the famous Lake Königssee joins the river Salzach just south of Salzburg. In summer, many local people come to its gravel banks and shallow bathing coves, and in its lower section – close to the Salzach – you can find several nudist areas

→ **Directions:**
Approaching from Salzburg, pass the roundabout by the supermarket, turn into Sonystraße and park behind a gas filling factory close to the river.

→ **GPS:** 47.73008, 13.07372

PRETTY AND STILL ACCESSIBLE –
Almkanal, Salzburg

The Almkanal takes its water from the river Königsseeache. When Salzburg was still ruled by the archbishops, this canal fed water to the mills, animal troughs and fountains of Mozart's city. Today, the "Alm" is used for generating power, as well as serving as an urban swimming and surfing spot.

→ **Directions:**
Exit the A10 at Salzburg-Süd and drive in the direction of Hellbrunn Palace. At the palace, turn left into Keltenallee until you get to Berchtesgadnerstraße. Turn right and follow the road to the Kommunalfriedhof cemetery. Park at the Hölle inn. From here, it is a few minutes walking time on Georg-Niko-laus-von-Nissen-Straße to the Almkanal.

→ **GPS:** 47.78092, 13.04198

13

a b

RIVER BEACH WITH BRIDGE AND "DIVING TOWER" –

Golling waterfall and Bluntautal, Golling

This waterfall (a) in Torren, which is part of the village of Golling, cascades in two steps over a total height of 75m. The water is chilly all year round because it surfaces as a mighty spring directly by the fall. The chargeable waterfall trail is open from May to the end of October. The 15-minute hike into the nearby Bluntautal valley (b) is also recommended.

→ **Directions:**
Exit the A10 at Golling and drive in the direction of the railway station. At the railway gate, turn left and follow the road to the bridge over the river Salzach. Having crossed the bridge, follow the signs to the waterfall.

→ **GPS:** a) 47.60113, 13.13691, b) 47.56666, 13.10008

a)

14

SALZKAMMERGUT
MOUNTAINS

Glasenbachklamm, Elsbethen

Depending on the water level of the Klausbach
stream, this gorge close to the edge of the
city of Salzburg offers good pools for a dip.
Following a fossil trail, visitors take a slightly
ascending hike to the hamlet of Höhenwald, with
its popular pub that attracts many day-trippers.

→ **Directions:**
Coming from Salzburg, 100m after the stone bridge over the Klausbach stream, turn left and
follow the signs to Glasenbachklamm.

→ **GPS:** 47.76769, 13.09690

15

AT TIMES, "SMALL" CAN BE BEAUTIFUL TOO –
Plötz waterfall, Ebenau

Starting at the car park, the child-friendly hike
leads along the Rettenbach stream and five
historic peasant mills to the 50m-tall waterfall.
Its plunge pool is easy to access, well suited for
bathing and very popular on hot summer days.

→ **Directions:**
Exit the A10 at Hallein and drive in the direction of Wiestal (Route L107). A few kilometres after
Ebenau, you will notice some large wooden figures on your left that point to the "Naturdenkmal
Plötz" (Plötz natural landmark). Park here.

→ **GPS:** 47.80057, 13.18210

16

SALZKAMMERGUT
MOUNTAINS

Felsenbad, Faistenau

This freely accessible and wildly romantic river bathing spot is one of only a handful in Austria. It is located above the Strüblweiher reservoir and offers rocky sunbathing spots as well as bathing pools of different sizes.

→ **Directions:**
Approaching from the south, take the Wiestal-Landesstraße (Route L107) to Faistenau. Coming from the north, follow the Wolfgangsee main road (Route B158). Following the signs to Lake "Hintersee", you will pass the natural swimming pool ahead of the lake.

→ **GPS:** 47.76388, 13.22762

NOT JUST THE FISHERMAN'S FRIEND –
Hintersee, Faistenau

In contrast to the Felsenbad (16), the neighbouring Lake Hintersee is suitable for swimming greater distances. The public bathing spots and shore areas along the pushchair-friendly 5km trail around the lake provide various entry points and spots for relaxation.

→ **Directions:**
For directions, see spot 16.

→ **GPS:** 47.75290, 13.24510

A 45-minute, moderately steep hike leads from the car park to this lake. In the Salzkammergut Indian summer, incredibly colourful broad-leaved trees are mirrored in the crystal-clear water.

→ **Directions:**
For directions, see spot 18. After Fuschl, continue on Route B158 for approx. 4km, direction St Gilgen, until you get to a small chapel.

→ **GPS:** 47.79936, 13.34357

19

ENCHANTING AND FAMILY-FRIENDLY –
Filbingsee, Fuschl

Apart from a rustic wooden table, this lake has
no facilities whatsoever, which means it is a
wonderful place for a retreat. The steep, direct
access to the lake offers magnificent views of
Lake Fuschlsee.

→ **Directions:**
Exit the A1 at Thalgau and take the Wolfgangseestraße (Route B158), direction Fuschl. When you
get to Brunn, a part of Fuschl, you will notice a joinery on your right. Park behind the joinery.

→ **GPS:** 47.78399, 13.27631

20
a b c

SALZKAMMERGUT
MOUNTAINS

Wiestal Valley

The Wiestal valley between Hallein and Ebenau is a true wild-swimming eldorado. There is a beautiful spot at the Hammerwirt weir (a) near the ancient Celtic city of Hallein. There is also the Almbachklamm gorge (b) a little further upstream. It is known for canyoning and is located directly below the reservoir dam of Lake Wiestalsee (c). The Wiestalsee itself offers plenty of space, even for more ambitious swimmers.

→ **Directions:**
Exit the A10 at Hallein and follow the Wiestal-Landesstraße (Route L107), direction Ebenau.

→ **GPS:** a) 47.70107, 13.11249
b) 47.73278, 13.15122
c) 47.75306, 13.17623

c)

b)

a)

21

KNOWN GORGE, UNKNOWN RIVER –
Gimbach Cascades,
Steinbach am Attersee

Here you can explore a meandering river with
passages and cascades of various sizes that
have been deeply carved into the rock. Depending on the previous days' weather and the
amount of rainfall, the stream has either a green
or yellow shine.

→ **Directions:**
An easy hike takes you from the car park at Gimbach-Kaskaden on Route B153, between Weißen-
bach and Mitterweißenbach, to the cascades.

→ **GPS:** 47.78943, 13.58923

Underground springs are the reason why the
lake's water table has a large seasonal variation
of several metres. The surrounding nature
reserve is home to a wealth of mushrooms
and berries.

→ **Directions:**
 Exit the A1 at Thalgau and follow the Wolfgangsee-Straße (Route B158), direction Bad Ischl/
 Ramsau.

→ **GPS:** 47.70342, 13.56943

23

SALZKAMMERGUT
MOUNTAINS

A GEOLOGICAL FAVOURITE –
Rettenbach, Bad Ischl

Walking past pretty pools, in 15 minutes you
reach Rettenbach mill and a bridge. Shortly
after, a commemorative plaque serves as a
reminder of ancestors of the Russian astronaut
Gagarin, who tragically drowned at this spot
when bathing.

→ **Directions:**
The wilderness of Rettenbach is reached by car or bus from Bad Ischl (see spot 22), via Steinfeld-
straße or Rettenbachwaldstraße.

→ **GPS:** 47.70775, 13.64061

Offensee, Ebensee

Crystal-clear water, beautiful bathing spots, magnificent mountain panoramas, a pushchair-friendly lake trail and two catering facilities. All of this is offered by Lake Offensee, which is 900m long and up to 38m deep.

→ **Directions:**
Exit the A1 at Gmunden and follow Route B145, direction Traunkirchen and Ebensee. Take the turn shortly thereafter.

→ **GPS:** 47.75100, 13.84185

OFF THE BEATEN TRACK –
Vorderer Langbathsee, Ebensee

The mountain giants of the Höllengebirge are impressively mirrored in Lake Langbathsee, which is framed by forest. Both lakes have marvellous natural bathing spots.

→ **Directions:**
For directions to Ebensee, see spot 24. The anterior lake can be reached by car from Ebensee, whereas the posterior Langbathsee is only accessible on foot or by bike.

→ **GPS:** 47.83483, 13.68826

UPPER
AUSTRIAN
PREALPS

UNCOMPLICATED WILD-SWIMMING FUN –
Rötelsee, Traunkirchen

This cave lake is not very big and not easy to get to. Access requires a boat taxi, a good sense of direction, surefootedness, good lighting and a few precautions. For information about guided tours on this unique adventure, please email h.ransmayr@me.com.

→ **Directions:**
For directions, see spot 24. Once you have arrived in Traunkirchen, park by the jetty.

→ **GPS:** 47.82046, 13.80735

The northern shore is suitable for swimming, provided that you don't mind the chilly water temperatures, even in summer. Catering facilities are located on the southern shore. Here, the road ends. There is a car park from which numerous trails lead into the nature reserve.

→ **Directions:**
Exit the A1 at Vorchdorf or the A9 at Ried im Traunkreis. The distance to the lake is approx. 10 kilometres for each option.

→ **GPS:** 47.74614, 13.95006

A "HEARTY" PLEASURE –
Traunfall, Roitham

In summer, people don't just swim here but also snorkel in the crystal-clear water. Please take note that, due to its steep banks, and depending on the water level and the weather, the Traunfall waterfall is not without its hazards for swimmers. Cliff-diving has also resulted in some serious accidents over the years!

→ **Directions:**
The proximity to the A1 (exit Laakirchen, direction Desselbrunn) makes the Traunfall easily accessible. Park by the bridge upstream of the fall.

→ **GPS:** 48.01810, 13.80121

IMPOSING FINALE OF THE LOGAR VALLEY –
Vorderer Gosausee, Gosau

In summer, the "eye of God", as this lake is called, is visited by thousands of tourists. It is also recommended to make the ascent with the Gosaukamm cable car or to hike to the "Hinterer" Gosausee (that is, the posterior lake). Compared with its big sister, it is much quieter here. There are lovely bathing spots for hardy swimmers at both lakes.

→ **Directions:**
The approach to the Ausseerland (the region around Aussee, where spots 31, 32 and 33 are located) and the Upper Austrian Salzkammergut (spots 29 and 30) is from the north. Exit the A1 at Regau and drive to Gmunden. Continue on Route B145 to Bad Ischl and Bad Goisern. Here, take the respective turnings to Ausseerland, Hallstatt and Gosau. If you are coming from the south, exit the A9 at Liezen and drive to the Trautenfels junction. Here, take the turning to Ausseerland, Bad Goisern and Gosau. Coming from the west, exit the A10 at Golling and continue on Route B162, direction Lammertal, through Abtenau to Gosau. From here, continue to Hallstätter See on Route B166, direction Bad Goisern, via Route B145 to Bad Aussee.

→ **GPS:** 47.53203, 13.49785

Hallstätter See, Obertraun

There are a few wild bathing spots near the
lakeside road between Hallstatt and Obertraun. Obertraun has a free bathing beach with
facilities.

→ **Directions:**
For directions, see spot 29.

→ **GPS:** 47.54670, 13.66604

31

TOTES
GEBIRGE

FOR THE SPORTY –

Ranftmühle, Grundlsee

This is a romantic spot for a brief, refreshing dip
or, with the natural counter-current facility, for
cold-water swimming as well. Park in the big car
park in Gössl, from which a leisurely 10-minute
walk leads to the mill.

→ **Directions:**
For directions, see spot 29.

→ **GPS:** 47.63508, 13.90414

The Nazis discarded a large number of counter-feit British sterling notes in this lake, and there has been speculation that they dumped other valuables here too. Whatever the history, the deep Lake Toplitz is a natural gem. From the car park in Gössl, it takes about 20 minutes to hike to the "Fischerhütte" inn (fishermen's hut).

→ **Directions:**
For directions, see spot 29. www.toplitzsee.at

→ **GPS:** 47.64355, 13.92316

33
TOTES GEBIRGE

a
b

A GLAMOROUS FOREST LAKE –

Altausseersee and Augstsee, Altaussee

Lake Altausseer See (a), crystal-clear and abundant in fish, is by the village of the same name at an altitude of 700m at the foot of the mighty Losermassiv. From an even and pushchair-friendly circular walk you can enjoy unforgettable views of the surrounding mountain peaks. The lake offers a large selection of idyllic bathing spots. It takes about a quarter of an hour to hike from the Loser mountain restaurant to Lake Augstsee (b), towered over by the pyramidal peak of the Atterkogel. Since the small lake is a mere 10m deep, it is pleasantly refreshing for bathing in summer.

→ **Directions:**
For directions to Bad Aussee, see spot 29. Then continue to Altaussee. From here, the Loser Mautstraße (toll road) leads to the mountain restaurant at approx. 1,600m above sea level.

→ **GPS:** a) 7.64197, 13.77479, b) 47.66306, 13.78702

b)

SIMPLY IDYLLIC –
Ödensee, Kainisch

34
DACHSTEIN MOUNTAINS

Despite being one of the smaller lakes in the Salzkammergut region, the 20-hectare Lake Ödensee, surrounded by dense mountain forest, is a popular bathing destination. Park by the comfortable Kohlröserlhütte, which has catering facilities. From here you can access many pretty bathing spots along a pushchair-friendly lake trail.

→ **Directions:**
   In Kainisch, turn off Route B145, which connects Grundlsee and Bad Mitterdorf.

→ **GPS:** 47.56328, 13.81993

Over thousands of years, the river Taugl
has deeply carved into the rock and formed
fantastic gorges, waterfalls and gravel banks.
The most popular bathing spots are to be found
below the *"Römerbrücke"* (Roman bridge).

→ **Directions:**
Exit the A10 at Hallein and follow the signs to Bad Vigaun and the Römerbrücke.

→ **GPS:** 47.66083, 13.15503

THE MAGNIFICENT SEVEN –
Seewaldsee, Sankt Koloman

This nature reserve at 1,000m is characterised
by alpine meadows and forest, as well as the
imposing presence of the Trattberg mountain.

→ **Directions:**
From the Salzach valley from Bad Vigaun or Golling via St Koloman. The nearest car park charges
a fee, but another car park, 20 minutes away, is free.

→ **GPS:** 47.62744, 13.27576

Lammer and Aubach, Voglau

Approx. 5km above the Lammeröfen, the Aubach stream joins the river from the left. Shortly before that is a big car park on the right, very close to the Lammerstrand (a).

Wade through the river Lammer and walk upstream along the Aubach to get to the big natural pool below the Aubach waterfall (b).

→ **Directions:**
   Exit the A10 at Golling and follow Route B162, direction Abtenau.

→ **GPS:** a), b) 47.59498, 13.29750

b)

38

TENNAN
MOUNTAINS

Wengsee, Werfenweng

Depending on the season, Lake Wengsee either is freely accessible or can be enjoyed for a small fee. Either way, you have great views of the Tennengebirge mountain range. We recommend that you get something to eat in the Seealmstüberl restaurant.

→ **Directions:**
Exit the A10 at Werfe/Pfarrwerfen and continue on Route L229 to Werfenweng. Follow the signs to Wengerau/Wengsee.

→ **GPS:** 47.46471, 13.25584

Bischofshofen Resort

Bischofshofen in the Salzach valley is known as a shopping destination. However, it is also the final stop of the famous Four Hills Tournament and an intermediate stop for a bicycle tour through the Tauern mountain range.

Bicyclists love to take a break, cool down and swim in the freely accessible bathing lake. From here, you get the most beautiful views of the mighty Tennen mountains.

→ **Directions:**
Follow the A10 to Bischofshofen and park by the tennis courts. From here, a pushchair-friendly trail crosses the bridge over the river Salzach and leads to the resort area.

→ **GPS:** 47.42936, 13.21708

Jägersee and Neuer See, Kleinarl

Park by the Jägersee inn. Here you can bathe
(a), hire a rowing boat and get something to eat.
You can also hike to Lake Tappenkarsee, which
is at a higher altitude and is one of the biggest
mountain lakes in the Eastern Alps. Considerab-
ly smaller is the "Neuer See" (new lake) between
Kleinarl and Jägersee, where swimming is now
sadly prohibited. This lake was created in 2017
as a result of a landslide (b).

→ **Directions:**
Exit the A10 at Flachau and follow the Wagrainer Straße (Route B163) to Wagrain. Then turn left,
direction Kleinarl/Jägersee.

→ **GPS:** a), b) 7.23617, 13.33073

b)

Palfnersee, Bad Gastein

Let the Graukogel chairlift carry you up to an altitude of 1,950m. From here, an approx. 1-hour hike through Arolla pine forest leads to Lake Palfnersee, which is 100m above your starting point. This walk is especially pretty in early summer when the "*alpenrosen*" are in full bloom, a species between rhododendron and azalea.

→ **Directions:**
At Lend, turn off Pinzgauer Straße (Route B311), direction Bad Gastein. At the southern end of the village, follow the signs to Graukogel.

→ **GPS:** 47.09044, 13.16456

Oberer Bockhartsee, Sportgastein

From the Valeriehaus restaurant, it is a 1-hour ascent to the Bockhartseehütte chalet, which is in a beautiful location. To get there, you can choose either the power station road or the steeper footpath. Passing the dammed, and less inviting, "Unterer Bockhartsee" (that is, the lower lake), it is another hour's hike to the "Oberer Bockhartsee" (the upper lake) at approx. 2,000m. The upper lake is relatively shallow, which also means it is pleasantly "warm" for bathing. Here, you will find the idyllic Austrian *alm*.

→ **Directions:**
For directions, see spot 41. Then continue to Sportgastein via a toll road that branches off the main road between Bad Gastein and Böckstein.

→ **GPS:** 47.08127, 13.03370

c)

b)

Grossarler Ache and Ötzelsee and Schödersee, Hüttschlag

a
b
c

43
ANKOGEL
GROUP

From the Talwirt restaurant it takes 20 minutes on foot to reach a small bridge with a pretty bathing spot (a) and a natural counter-current facility. Immediately nearby are Lake Ötzelsee (b) and a small Kneipp facility for the water-based treatment of certain illnesses. This is also the starting point for the approx. 1-hour ascent to the periodic Lake Schödersee (c). The track leads along a rushing mountain stream. However, this stream only exists during the thawing period, when the snow is melting, or after prolonged rainfall. Hardy swimmers are then able to enjoy unique swimming experiences above flowering alpine meadows.

→ **Directions:**
Take the turning off Pinzgauer Straße (Route B311) in St Johann and follow Route Alpendorf-Straße until you have passed Hüttschlag, a village in the national park.

→ **GPS:** a), b) 47.13473, 13.29156, c) 47.11268, 13.31976

a)

b)

Fallertümpfe and Blauer Tumpf, Gmünd

The drive through the Malta valley leads past numerous mountain streams and waterfalls. The descent to the Fallertümpfe is not easy, but you will be rewarded by the experience of swimming in a fantastic natural pool (a) and a waterfall. A few kilometres upstream of the Fallertümpfe on the left-hand side of the road is a car park with a sign pointing to the Blauer Tumpf (b). The well-established trail to this pool takes 10 minutes. When you get there, you will be surprised by what a wonderful swimming spot it is, and how truly epic in size.

→ **Directions:**
Exit the A10 at Gmünd and follow the signs to the 14km toll road into the Malta valley.

→ **GPS:** a) 47.01355, 13.43278, b) 47.02898, 13.39197

a)

Kočevje mining lake

This natural gem is surrounded by wonderfully spongy quaking bog. The lake is located on the Hochgosch ridge between the southern shore of Lake Millstatt and the lower Drava valley.
The trail to this romantic marsh lake starts at the restaurant's car park and takes approx. 15 minutes. As an option, there is also a nice Kneipp trail for the water-based treatment of various illnesses.

→ **Directions:**
  Exit the A10 at Spittal an der Drau-Ost. At the second roundabout, drive in the direction of Egelsee via Molzbichl until you get to the Lug ins Land inn.

→ **GPS:** 46.78425, 13.56066

BIG SPRING, SHORT RIVER –

Almsee, Filzmoos

The Hofalmen farmsteads below the Filzmoos Almsee have often been used as a location for films and TV adverts. The not very dense forest and green alpine meadows below the characteristic peak of the Bischofsmütze present the perfect mountain idyll. This rather chilly alpine lake is fed by a mountain stream. The hike from the car park takes approx. 10 minutes.

→ **Directions:**
Exit the A10 at Eben and continue to Filzmoos. Then take the toll road that leads up to the alpine terrain.

→ **GPS:** 47.47848, 13.53369

Zauchensee, Altenmarkt

Waterskiing can be on the cards here by springtime, when the slopes of this Skiing World Cup location are still covered in snow but Lake Zauchensee is no longer frozen. However, Lake Zauchensee is also very attractive in summer due to its location in a hiker's paradise.

→ **Directions:**
Exit the A10 at Altenmarkt. From the centre of the village, it is an approx. 15-minute drive to the Zauchensee.

→ **GPS:** 47.29826, 13.45658

48) Tauernkarsee (next page)

48

RADSTADT
TAUERN

Tauernkarsee, Untertauern

This lake at 1,700m is surrounded by high alpine forest. It is particularly beautiful in autumn when the larches are on fire with their spectacular orange, brown and yellow hues. However, if you would like to try the gourmet specialities at nearby Tauernkaralm, it is advisable to visit in early autumn.

→ **Directions:**
  Exit the A10 at Altenmarkt and drive via Radstadt to the northern edge of the Tauern Pass. The 4-km dirt road to the Tauernkaralm starts 200m after the turning to Gnadenalm.

→ **GPS:** 47.28425, 13.52210

Krummschnabelsee, Obertauern

49

RADSTADT
TAUERN

It is nice to swim in this small mountain lake, which is reasonably warm in summer, as part of a three-lakes mountain-bike or hiking tour. Starting this 8.5km tour on the summit of the pass, follow the Seekarstraße, direction Seekarhaus. Continue through Hundsfeldmoor marsh, past Lake Hundsfeldsee to Diktn Alm.

From here – and a little steeper – ascend to the highest point of the hike: Lake Krummschnabelsee. After your wild-swimming break, descend to the inviting Hochalm at Lake Günwaldsee and return to your starting point via the Fluhbachalm.

→ **Directions:**
For directions, see spot 48. From here it is approx. 10km to the summit of the Tauern Pass.

→ **GPS:** 47.26327, 13.54918

Prebersee, Tamsweg

The dark colouring of this mountain lake is due to suspended particles from the marsh, and these also allow for the known "Preberschie-ßen". The aim of this shooting competition is to hit a target with bullets that bounce off the surface of the water. Bathing is only permitted at the defined access areas.

→ **Directions:**
   Exit the A10 at Rennweg. The drive to Tamsweg takes approx. 20 minutes, and from there a short mountain road leads to the lake.

→ **GPS:** 47.18496, 13.85855

Duisitzkarsee, Schladming

The walk on trail 775 and past the imposing waterfall of the Duisitzkar stream is steep and challenging, but you gain height quickly. After half an hour, you leave the high alpine forest behind. Ahead of you, a magnificent panorama unfolds with a picture-perfect mountain lake, and the Duisitzkarsee and Fahrlech chalets offer well-deserved food and drink.

→ **Directions:**
  Follow the Enns valley main road (Route B320) to the Skiing World Cup town of Schladming. Continue to the Rohrmoos/Obertal area of the town and park the car by the Eschachalm.

→ **GPS:** 47.29875, 13.69151

52

a
b

SCHLADMING
TAVERN

A SPOT FOR NATURE LOVERS AND POETS –
Hüttensee and Obersee, Aich

The hike leads past Lake Bodensee, where swimming is sadly not permitted, towards the end of the valley. Continue on a steep 1-hour ascent to lake Hüttensee (a). Here the idyllic Hans-Wödl-Hütte lodge awaits, offering food, drink and accommodation. Another 45 minutes from here, at approx. 1,700m and in a wonderfully quiet and peaceful setting, is the dreamy Lake Obersee (b). Along the way to Lake Obersee is a very impressive waterfall, which you can swim in.

→ **Directions:**
  Approach from the Enns valley main road (Route B320) from Ruperting or Aich and continue via the toll road into the Seewig valley until you get to the car park.

→ **GPS:** a) 47.35957, 13.81715, b) 47.35198, 13.81681

a)

WOULD YOU LIKE ANYTHING ELSE, SIR/MADAM? –

Spechtensee, Wörschach

The water quality of this small marsh lake is excellent and it is pleasantly warm for bathing. The Lake Spechtensee nature reserve offers numerous hiking trails, one of which leads to the picturesque Wörschachklamm gorge.

→ **Directions:**
In Tauplitz, turn off Route B145, which connects Grundlsee and Bad Mitterdorf, and follow the track to the lake.

→ **GPS:** 47.55965, 14.09787

ONCE ABANDONED, NOW HIGHLY POPULAR –
Sulzkarsee, Hieflau

The Sulzkaralm promises ample reward for those who don't shy away from the arduous ascent through the steep wilderness of the Hartelsgraben rift. The *alm* is fabulous alpine meadow terrain, and you will find the highly recommended Almhütte chalet (only open at summer weekends) and Lake Sulzkarsee. This is the only natural lake in the Gesäuse National Park.

→ **Directions:**
Approaching from the north, exit the A1 at Ybbs-Wieselburg and follow the Erlauftalstraße (Route B25) to Mooslandl. Continue on Route B115 to Hieflau and take Route B146 to the Hartelsgraben. Also take Route B146 if you are approaching from the west via Liezen from the Enns valley.

→ **GPS:** 47.56021, 14.68120

GIGANTIC BATHING AND CLIMBING –
Josersee, St Ilgen

In approx. 90 minutes, trail 839 leads via the
Heinzler-Alm and Joser-Alm to the enchanting
Lake Josersee, the surface of which mirrors the
peak of the Hochschwab.

→ **Directions:**
Approach by car via Kapfenberg, St Marein, or from Mariazell (Route B20) via Seeberg and
Seewiesen to Thörl. From here, follow the signs to the Gasthof Bodenbauer restaurant through
St Ilgen to the hiking car park.

→ **GPS:** 47.57886, 15.07471

With a length of 60km, the Styrian Salza is one of the longest unspoilt wild rivers in Europe. It therefore has a wide variety of suitable bathing spots. The kayak jetties at the mouth of the river Lassing, below the tall bridge in Palfau, and at the Wasserlochklamm gorge suspension bridge are very popular, and also very crowded.

→ **Directions:**
Exit the A1 at Ybbs-Wieselburg and follow the Erlauftalstraße (Route B25) via Göstling (Route B56) to Erzhalden/Palfau. Here, turn left via Salzatalstraße (Route B24) to Wildalpen.

→ **GPS:** 47.68542, 14.92615

57

GÖSTLING
ALPS

Ybbs, Göstling

The river Ybbs is not just loved by fly fishers but also extremely popular with bathers because of its superb water quality. The bathing spot shown here is in the village but there are many other beautiful places for swimming downstream between Göstling and Waidhofen.

→ **Directions:**
For directions, see spot 56.

→ **GPS:** 47.81103, 14.93337

58 a b c

STRAIGHT INTO THE EYE –
Ötschergräben, Mittenbach

TÜRNITZ
ALPS

"Austria's Grand Canyon." The Ötscher Nature Park offers more possibilities for gorge explorers and wild swimmers than could possibly be covered in detail in this guide. One option is to explore the route from Mitterbach via the Erlaufklause to Ötscher and Hias. This is one of many trails and can easily be combined with a journey on the Mariazell Railway. For further information, visit www.naturpark-oetscher.at/die-oetschergraeben.

→ **Directions:**
Exit the A1 at St Pölten and follow Mariazeller Straße (Route B20) to Mitterbach, which should take half an hour.

→ **GPS:** a) 47.84470, 15.24832, b) 47.84413, 15.25579, c) 47.84385, 15.26394

c)

GERMANY

MUCH MORE THAN JUST HOLIDAY COASTLINES, BEACHES AND ISLANDS

Bavaria is a paradise for wild swimmers. Wonderful spots are found not only in the Bavarian Alps, which are part of the northern Eastern Alps, but also in the Bavarian Prealps and the foothills of the Alps. Thousands of years ago, the alpine glaciers stretched much further, towards the north of Bavaria. When the masses of ice melted, they left many lovely lakes behind in the Bavarian Prealps, some of them forming entire lake districts. In addition, Bavaria offers wild-swimming enthusiasts magnificent waterfalls, clean mountain streams and enchanting stretches of wild riverbanks.

(85b) Obersee

59

ALLGÄU
ALPS

FRESHWATER POOLS WITH A SEA VIEW –

Buchenegg waterfalls, Oberstaufen

Over thousands of years, the Weißach river has carved a spectacular course through the Nagelfluhkette mountain range. Today, its rushing waters form the two pools that have become one of the oldest water parks in Germany. It is a special adventure to dip into the pools from a diving height of approx. 30m. This highly risky challenge is called "*jucken*" in Allgäu dialect, meaning "to jump". In recent years, it has become enormously popular, and not just with the local youth. For those who can live without the adrenaline kick, the lower plunge pool, with 20m diameter and shallow banks, offers a place for cooling off. However, the temperature only reaches about 16°C, even in high summer.

→ **Directions:**
Approaching from the town of Immenstadt, drive via the roundabout at the Hündle mountain railway, direction Hinterstaufen/Buchenegg. Coming from Oberstaufen, at the railway station, take the turning to Bad Rain/Buchenegg. From the car park (which charges), the hike to the waterfalls via a steep zigzag path takes 20 minutes.

→ **GPS:** 47.52973, 10.04984

60

FULL OF LIFE –
Kögelweiher, Nesselwang

This 10-hectare marsh pond is in a quiet location off the beaten track, approx. 4km from Nesselwang. It is a romantic setting, with the pond being embedded between forest, meadows and green hills. Despite the marshy shores in certain areas, those who follow the pretty footpath from the car park in the forest will discover at least three suitable bathing spots.

→ **Directions:**
The Kögelweiher pond, with its pleasant temperature, is best reached from Nesselwand im Allgäu via Hertingen, either by foot, bicycle or car.

→ **GPS:** 47.62321, 10.54985

61

LAND'S END –

Schwansee, Alpsee, Schwangau

AMMERGAU
ALPS

Swimming with a view of Neuschwanstein Castle. This is what you can enjoy at the bathing spot at Lake Schwansee (a), near the royal castles of Hohenschwangau and Neuschwanstein, approx. 400m north of Lake Alpsee (b). The lake is not particularly deep and so warms up quickly. It is therefore more popular than the other bathing lakes in the Schwangau region – Alpsee, Bannwaldsee and the Forggensee reservoir, which is only recommended from late summer.

→ **Directions:**
When you follow the crowds of tourists or the signs to the fairytale castles from the town of Füssen, you can't miss Lake Schwansee. Just before you get to the castles, on the approach, the car park is in the wood to your right. From here, it is 500m walking distance to the lake.

→ **GPS:** a), b) 47.55813, 10.72117

b)

A GRAVELLY ADVENTURE –
Schwaigsee, Wildsteig

AMMERGAU
ALPS

Due to its good water quality and generally mild temperature, swimming in this marsh lake at an altitude of 830m is a sheer pleasure. In addition, not only the bathing but also the parking by the kiosk are free of charge.

→ **Directions:**
Due to the lake's location next to Steingadener Straße between Wildsteig and Rottenbuch, access by car is easy and stress-free.

→ **GPS:** 47.70797, 10.95884

63

SWIMMING UNDER BIRCHES –

Ammerdurchbruch
Scheibum, Saulgrub

The Ammer valley is regarded as one of the most beautiful unspoilt river valleys in the Northern Limestone Alps. A mere 15km north of its source, this young mountain river, over aeons of time, broke through a rocky ridge between Altenau and Peißenberg, carving the "Scheibum" or Ammer gorge, which today is a protected area. The characteristic gorge section, where the river broke through, starts below the bridge by the Kammerl power station. It is approx. 600m long and offers marvellous possibilities for river bathing.

→ **Directions:**
Access to the Scheibum is via Route B23 to Saulgrub and from there via Achelestraße.

→ **GPS:** 47.66232, 10.98791

SPRING EXPLORATION FOR OLMS –
"CAVE SWIMMING" AT

Eibsee, Grainau

This crystal-clear mountain lake, which is privately owned by the Eibsee Hotel, is at an altitude of 1,000m at the foot of the Zugspitze, Germany's highest mountain, and approx. 13km from Garmisch-Partenkirchen. It is noteworthy that

Lake Eibsee has several islands, which means that island-hopping with a view of the Zugspitze is possible, be it by swimming or with one of the boats or SUPs that are available for hire.

→ **Directions:**
A journey on one of the last remaining cogwheel railways in Germany, from Garmisch-Partenkirchen, is a unique experience. It takes half an hour to the lake. The road also follows the railway line.

→ **GPS:** 47.45498, 10.98313

65

WETTERSTEIN
AND MIEMING
RANGE

Geroldsee, Gerold

This marsh lake has shallow shores and reasonable bathing temperatures, which also make it suitable for children. Its panoramic view makes it one of the most scenic lakes in the Karwendel mountains. The western and northern shores are lined by flat meadows, and it is here where you find the fenced-in bathing beach that in summer can be used for a small fee. The lake can also be accessed from its southern shore via an undulating mountain meadow.

→ **Directions:**
To get to the lake, park in the car park by Route B2, leading from Garmisch-Partenkirchen to Mittenwald, and walk the 600m distance via a beaten track.

→ **GPS:** 47.49278, 11.21827

66
SOMEWHERE IN NO MAN'S LAND –
Lautersee, Mittenwald

WETTERSTEIN
AND MIEMING
RANGE

Lake Lautersee, which is 12 hectares in size
and up to 19m deep, is located on a wooded
high alpine plateau at an altitude of 1,000m.
Its location is above the town of Mittenwald
at the foot of the Hoher Kranzberg mountain.
The lake features a hotel, a small public bathing
section and a boat hire facility. There are freely
accessible bathing spots on the lake's southern
and eastern shores.

→ **Directions:**
Approaching via the A95 from Munich to Garmisch-Partenkirchen, follow Route B11 from Munich
to Innsbruck and the Brenner Pass. Otherwise, take the "Deutsche Alpenstraße" (German Alpine
Road), Route B23, from Oberammergau to Garmisch-Partenkirchen and Bad Tölz.

→ **GPS:** 47.43693, 11.23837

67

FOOTHILLS OF
THE BAVARIAN
ALPS

CITY LAKE FOR OUTDOOR-SPORTS LOVERS –
River Danube, Kelheim

The Danube is not just an important waterway but also provides marvellous bathing spots on hot summer days. Some of the most beautiful spots are to be found between Kelheim and Weltenburg. It is best to ask the friendly staff of the tourist information board in Kelheim for details about the bathing spots at the Lange Wand, the "Kanuinsel" (canoe island) or on other Danube beaches. You will be able to obtain up-to-date information about the Danube's water levels and about possible hazards. This is important because the river's currents are often difficult to judge, and also the significant shipping traffic on the Danube means that swimming is not without its risks for the inexperienced and for children.

→ **Directions:**
   Exit the A9 (Nuremberg–Munich), the A3 (Nuremberg–Passau) or the A93 (intersection Haller-tau–Regensburg) at Kelheim and continue on Route St2233 to Weltenburg.

→ **GPS:** 48.89572, 11.81982

68

URBAN SWIMMING AND EVENT VENUE –

Hofstättersee, Prutting

Dense areas of reed and forest only allow access to the lake in certain places. The most recommended bathing site, which is also suitable for small children, is on the eastern shore by the Strandhaus kiosk. Here you can not only park but also get something to eat in the cosy beer garden while looking out onto the lake. The southern shore features an interesting marsh nature trail, the somewhat dilapidated wooden planks of which make pushchair access rather difficult.

→ **Directions:**
When approaching from the motorway Munich–Salzburg, continue via Stephanskirchen, direction Hub, until you get to the turning to the Strandhaus.

→ **GPS:** 47.898444, 12.172986

CLOSE TO THE WIND –
Happinger See, Happing

FOOTHILLS OF
THE BAVARIAN
ALPS

The area around the city of Rosenheim is home to a large number of small lakes, all of which have fabulous views of the Bavarian Alps, which seem to be almost within reach. The neighbouring bathing lakes Happinger Ausee and Floriansee are of particular interest to nudist bathers, as well as Happinger See, which is approx. 1.2km to the south-west. While the peninsula at Lake Ausee is used for nudist bathing, at Floriansee it is the northern shore and at Happinger See the eastern shore.

→ **Directions:**
Parking is possible at the kiosk and the bathing beach of Happinger See. Drive to the lake via Rosenheim and Raubling.

→ **GPS:** 47.83240, 12.14257

70

FOOTHILLS OF
THE BAVARIAN
ALPS

A KARST RIVER PAR EXCELLENCE –

Hochstrasser See, Thal

This is a small gravel quarry pond near the city of Rosenheim. Its northern shore features a pretty gravel beach with a sunbathing lawn, volleyball court and kiosk. From Thursday to Sunday in summer, this place becomes a Swiss-style raclette outlet. The noise from the nearby motorway Munich–Salzburg is slightly disturbing, but really only in spring and autumn when there are no leaves on the trees to provide a sound barrier.

→ **Directions:**
The bathing spot is free to use, whereas there is a fee for the car park. The spot is accessed via Route Staatsstraße 2359 from Rohrdorf to Thansau and then via Biedererstraße, or, coming from Neubeuern, via Thansauer Straße.

→ **GPS:** 47.80932, 12.13756

Langbürgner See and Pelhamer See

North-west of Lake Chiemsee are the villages of Eggstätt in the north-east and Hemhof in the west, the latter belonging to the parish of Bad Endorf. The Eggstätt-Hemhofer-Seenplatte (lake district) is named after these communities. This lake district includes 18 lakes with a total surface area of 3.5km². The biggest of these lakes, Langbürgner See, still offers more remote and unspoilt bathing spots, both on its southern shore in the lakeside wood (a) and in Thal and Hartmannsberg. The bathing spot at Pelhamer See (b) has a jetty and is freely accessible, with the nearby hotel offering delicious food.

→ **Directions:**
The region around Bad Endorf is reached in a few minutes by car from the motorway exit of the same name on the Salzburg–Munich motorway.

→ **GPS:** a) 47.89539, 12.36178,
   b) 47.93342, 12.34507

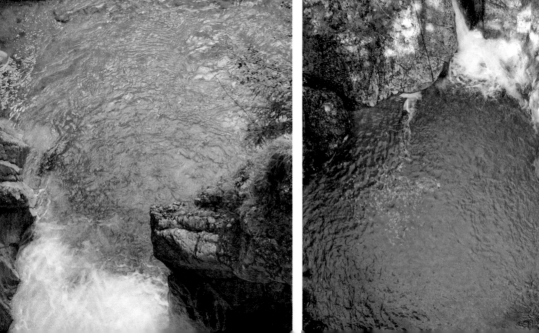

Tatzlwurm waterfalls, Oberaudorf

The hamlet of Tatzlwurm only really consists of the hotel Zum Feurigen Tatzlwurm and its adjacent buildings and car parks. The track to the waterfalls begins immediately behind the hotel. Swimming is possible in the plunge pool of the lower fall's cascade and in several pools further downstream.

→ **Directions:**
These falls, which are steeped in ancient legend, are accessed via Oberaudorf and the Tatzlwurmstraße toll road or, coming from the west, via the Sudelfeldstraße route. www.tatzlwurm.de

→ **GPS:** 47.67128, 12.08248

Chiemsee, Chieming

Lake Chiemsee features countless bathing spots, both wild and "civilised", so that one is spoilt for choice at the "Bavarian Sea", the name given to the lake because of its large size. Apart from the protected areas of the shore – for example, by the mouth and delta of the Tiroler Achen river, which is worth seeing – there are so many spots that you will always find a place for wild swimming. The bathing beach in Chieming is the easiest to reach from the Munich–Salzburg motorway (being only 6km from it), and it is also great for children. The lakeside promenade has playgrounds, beach volleyball courts and kiosks.

→ **Directions:**
Exit the A8 at Grabenstätt. At the roundabout, take the second exit to the right to Chieming (approx. 10km).

→ **GPS:** 47.88016, 12.53177

THE PERFECT PLACE TO FIND YOUR PEACE –
Reifinger See, Grassau

This lake is one of the few barrier-free bathing lakes in Bavaria. It features a disabled car park, a wheelchair-friendly changing room, a wheelchair WC and a hire wheelchair for the access ramp. The site is user-friendly in many other aspects as well, because car parks, sunbathing lawns, bathing jetty, area for small children, mud-crossing bridge, beach volleyball court and climbing island can all be used free of charge.

→ **Directions:**
Exit the A8 (Munich–Salzburg) at Bernau and continue on Route B305, direction Reit im Winkl, to Grassau (approx. 8km). From there, follow Kreisstraße Route TS45 to the lake.

→ **GPS:** 47.77360, 12.45985

This small bathing lake, which is particularly family-friendly, is located in a valley basin surrounded by forest below the peak of the Hochgern mountain. The well-kept bathing facility is freely accessible and has playgrounds and a kiosk where you can hire fishing rods.

→ **Directions:**
  Coming from the north, exit the Munich–Salzburg motorway at Bernau am Chiemsee. Follow Route B305 to Marquartstein and continue to Unterwössen. When approaching from the south via St Johann in Tirol or Kufstein/Walchsee, drive to Kössen and continue on Route B172/B305.

→ **GPS:** 47.72607, 12.47050

Alzbad, Truchtlaching

This river bathing section has substantial facilities and is also suitable for children, but be aware that there is no lifeguard on site. The river Alz drains Lake Chiemsee, which means that it has pleasant water temperatures. Depending on how you feel, you can either let yourself be carried by the current or swim against it.

→ **Directions:**
Approaching from Austria, exit the A8 at Grabenstätt. When travelling from Munich, exit the motorway at Bernau and follow the signs to Seeon-Seebruck. In Truchtlaching, turn off Chiemseestraße into Seeoner Straße, cross the river Alz and park on the left side by the bridge.

→ **GPS:** 47.96046, 12.49927

Höglwörther See, Anger

This small lake is in a picturesque location below the Augustinian monastery. If you are interested in geology, it is worth pointing out that this lake is a "terminal moraine" lake of the former Saalach glacier. Today, crayfish once again inhabit this body of water, a sure sign that the water quality is excellent. There are entry points to the water around the lake, where bathing is free of charge, as well as a small waterfall and, on the northern shore, a public bathing section including kiosk.

→ **Directions:**
King Ludwig I of Bavaria called Anger the "prettiest village in my kingdom". To get there, exit the A8 at Bad Reichenhall and follow the signs. The drive only takes a few minutes.

→ **GPS:** 47.81623, 12.84489

The nature reserve on the eastern shore offers a freely accessible bathing spot. In summer, the lake is surrounded by a sea of flowers, some of which are protected species. The water quality of this lake, which is largely fed underground, is superb, and the water temperatures are quite good for bathing.

→ Directions:
  The "Dreiseengebiet" (Three Lakes District) in the Eastern Chiemgau Alps nature reserve – which comprises the Weitsee, Mittersee and Lödensee – is in the immediate vicinity to the famous Deutsche Alpenstraße (German Alpine Road, B305) between Reit im Winkl and Ruhpolding.

→ **GPS:** 47.68615, 12.57058

Zwingsee, Inzell

The Max Aicher Arena in Inzell is regarded as
the Mecca of (ice) speed skating. Lake Zwingsee
is directly next to the arena, situated between
the Falkenstein and Kienbergerl mountains
and surrounded by forest. Coming from the
Max Aicher Arena, you initially reach a small
chargeable bathing facility. There is a hidden
wild-bathing spot a few hundred metres further
into the woods.

→ **Directions:**
   Inzell is approx. 11km from the Munich–Salzburg motorway. Exit the motorway at Traunstein/
   Siegsdorf and continue on Route B306.

→ **GPS:** 47.74923, 12.75102

Seeleiten
Buchwinkel

REACHING FOR THE SKY, IN HELL –
Waginger See, Waging am See

Lake Waginger See features numerous beach
bathing sections and campsites but only a
handful of spots where wild bathing is possible.
To get to the spot that is easiest to access,
drive from Waging towards Freilassing until you
see the sign to "Seeleiten, Buchwinkl" on your
right. Here there is a small parking bay. A beaten
track leads through the lakeside thicket to the
warmest bathing lake in Upper Bavaria.

→ **Directions:**
   Approach from the A8 (Munich–Salzburg) and take the exit at Traunstein/Siegsdorf, direction
   Traunstein. From there it is approx. 10km to Waging.

→ **GPS:** 47.93027, 12.77860

Weidsee, Petting

Lake Weidsee by Seehaus Castle is a true gem that requires a sensitive approach. A notice-board shows a code of conduct to preserve the lake's fragile beauty, reminding visitors to respect the environment and act responsibly. Since the nature reserve doesn't have a car park, it is recommended to walk or bicycle from the nearby hamlet of Ringham.

→ **Directions:**
   For directions to Petting, see spot 77 or 85. Petting is situated between those two locations.

→ **GPS:** 47.89961, 12.82191

Abtsdorfer See,
Saaldorf-Surheim

FOOTHILLS OF
THE BAVARIAN
ALPS

When the alpine glaciers melted about 10,000 years ago, a large lake district 30 x 10km was formed in the foothills of the Alps. Despite its ice-age past, Lake Abtsee is now one of the warmest bathing lakes in Bavaria, and also one of the most abundant in fish. There is a wooded island in the lake and beautiful bicycle and hiking trails surround the Abtsdorfer See. The lake has many wild-bathing spots and a beach bathing section with a campsite and a superb restaurant.

→ **Directions:**
To get to Lake Abtsee and nearby Laufen (82), exit the Munich–Salzburg motorway at Traunstein, Neukirchen or Bad Reichenhall.

→ **GPS:** 47.91568, 12.90361

The ancient border town of Laufen is proud of its panoramic location in the foothills of the Alps as well as its medieval, almost Italianate, flair and many sights of interest. For river swimmers, the beach on the river Salzach is another highlight. The beach is located by the characteristic serpentine with which the alpine river winds itself around the old town. You can become a "border swimmer" here, since the Austrian town of Oberndorf, famous as the birthplace of the carol "Silent Night", is on the opposite riverbank. The degree of difficulty for swimming is determined by the water level and the currents.

→ **Directions:**
For directions, see spot 81.

→ **GPS:** 47.94360, 12.93713

a)

b)

Königsbach waterfall and Malerwinkel

BERCHTESGADEN
ALPS

Park in the large chargeable car park at the foot of the Jenner mountain and follow the signs to "Malerwinkel" (painter's corner). From there, continue to the "Rabenwand" (rooks' wall). After an approx. 20-minute hike, which is moderately steep and offers great views, the official hiking trail comes to an end. However, for the adventurous and sure-footed (and only those!), a beaten track leads to the magnificent natural pools (a) of the Königsbach stream and, another 100m uphill, to a waterfall. Here, you need to proceed with the utmost caution and level-headedness. Please note that the direct descent by the Königsbach stream down to the Malerwinkel is slippery and hazardous. It is better to return the same way that you came so that you can enjoy a few moments of refreshing swimming fun in the truly picturesque Malerwinkel (b).

→ **Directions:**
You get to Schönau from the north, west or east via the A8 (Munich–Salzburg). Exit the motorway at Bad Reichenhall and follow Route B20 to and past Schönau. Approaching from the south on the Tauern motorway, exit at Salzburg Süd and follow Route B305 to Berchtesgaden. Then take Route B20 to and past Schönau.

→ **GPS:** (a), (b) 47.58258, 12.99357

b)

a)

Königssee-Salet, Obersee, Schönau am Königssee

In Schönau, embark on a journey on one of the electric boats that takes you past the pilgrimage church of St Bartholomä to Salet (a). From there, a hiking trail leads in the direction of Fischunkelalm. After only 10 minutes, you get to Lake Obersee (i.e. the "upper lake", spot b), which is the small sister of Lake Königssee. You can either dive into the water straight away or follow the trail, which is no longer pushchair-friendly, to Fischunkelalm, where you can get something to eat and drink. Then the trail leads to the 470m-tall Röthbach waterfall.

The scenery in the valley basin is so utterly magical that some might say it borders on kitsch.

→ **Directions:**
  For directions, see spot 84.

→ **GPS:** (a), (b) 47.58258, 12.99357

b)

This alpine idyll of a mountain lake and alpine forest, which has been photographed, painted and visited countless times, is approx. 4km west of Ramsau at an altitude of 790m. A circular track allows you to access many wild bathing spots, the most beautiful of which are on the edge of the "Zauberwald" (enchanted forest). Wild mountain streams, which both feed and drain the lake, ensure that the water quality is simply mesmerising. Temperatures, however, never rise above 15 to 16°C, even in summer. You can park the car near the hotel or in small parking bays in the forest.

→ **Directions:**

Lake Hintersee is a very popular destination. To get there, exit the A8 at Bad Reichenhall and continue on Routes B21/B20 via Berchtesgaden and Ramsau to Hintersee.

→ **GPS:** 47.60844, 12.85851

Thumsee, Bad Reichenhall

Sigmund Freud, the founder of psychoanalysis, came here with his family on vacation in summer, as Lake Thumsee is perfect for bathing and swimming. It is located in the nature reserve of the same name a few kilometres east of the alpine city of Bad Reichenhall. "Wild" bathing spots can be found near the Seewirt restaurant, where guests can sit on a beautiful lakeside terrace and enjoy the delicious food, in particular the fish. You can also park the car here, but do come early in high summer because spaces will fill up quickly.

→ **Directions:**
The lake is by the Staatsstraße St2101 route between Bad Reichenhall and Inzell. To get there, exit the Munich–Salzburg motorway at the respective junctions.

→ **GPS:** 47.71722, 12.81968

Almbachklamm, Marktschellenberg

The Almbach stream was developed to attract visitors by creating a trail system consisting of 29 bridges and planks as well as 320 steps and one tunnel. The gorge is open from early May to the end of October and grants you access to some wonderful pools. The most spectacular amongst them is by the waterfall right at the beginning of the gorge. Despite the plunge pool not being particularly deep, it is a unique experience to take a dip in this spot and let the water cascade down onto you.

→ **Directions:**
Marktschellenberg can be reached via the Munich–Salzburg motorway. Exit the motorway at Salzburg Süd (Grödig) and follow the "Deutsche Alpenstraße" (German Alpine Road), or drive via Bad Reichenhall and Berchtesgaden.

→ **GPS:** 47.66870, 13.02534

89

BERCHTESGADEN
ALPS

DEEPLY FASCINATING –
Berchtesgaden Ache, Marktschellenberg

In the centre of the village of Marktschellenberg, the road crosses the river Ache. Park
the car by the bridge and walk a few hundred
metres upstream to a small sports ground
where you find a sunbathing lawn and an entry
point. There is sufficient distance for swimming
up to the bridge but there is a weir immediately
thereafter. At normal water levels, the current is
harmless, and you can easily get out of the river
on the right-hand bank via small stone steps. We
recommend that you visit the lovely restaurant
with a terrace by the river on the left-hand bank.

→ **Directions:**
For directions, see spot 88.

→ **GPS:** 47.69519, 13.04495

Ausee, Freilassing

90

FOOTHILLS OF
THE BAVARIAN
ALPS

Freilassing is the German border town to the neighbouring city of Salzburg. The unspoilt water meadows by the river Saalach are a popular recreation area with local hikers, joggers and cyclists.

→ **Directions:**
  Coming from the border crossing, take the turning to Burghausen at the first crossroad, cross the Mühlbach stream and park the car approx. 200m thereafter by the first turning on the right. From here, it is a 5-minute walk to the natural bathing lake.

→ **GPS:** 47.84108, 12.99708

SWITZERLAND

A DECLARATION OF LOVE TO A
SMALL BUT FANTASTIC COUNTRY

The Swiss are known as passionate open-water swimmers. Just think of the enthusiasts who regularly swim the river Rhine in Basel, the river Limmat in Zurich or the Aare in Bern. Apart from these river bathing spots, which are steeped in tradition, the alpine republic of Switzerland offers many other fabulous spots for wild dipping or wild swimming. The descriptions in this guide begin in the west of the country and proceed eastward, as well as containing a final swimming spot in the Principality of Liechtenstein.

A LAKE MADE FOR WALKING IN WONDERFUL SCENERY –

Cascata del Bignasco

TICINO ALPS

The idyllic village of Bignasco is at the confluence of the rivers Maggia and Bavona at the
upper end of the Maggia valley. Apart from
various bicycle and hiking routes, there is also
the *"Cascata grande"* behind the small but well-
kept public swimming pool, where you can also
park the car. The waterfall is easy to reach and,
due to the rugged rocks and colourful flower
meadows, it is very popular with photographers.

→ **Directions:**
  For directions, see spot 94.

→ **GPS:** 46.33583, 8.61261

171

Giumaglio is an enchanting Ticino mountain village in the Maggia valley and features many old and beautiful houses with ancient stone roofs. The waterfall cannot be overlooked when standing in the centre of the village, and it is also easily accessible. For those who are seeking greater adventures, we recommend a canyoning tour through the Giumaglio gorge, with a subsequent abseil down the last waterfall (see canyonauten.de).

→ **Directions:**
For directions, see spot 94.

→ **GPS:** 46.27440, 8.68446

ALMOST A LITTLE SPOOKY –
Rio Salto, Maggia

When the sun is just in the right place – mostly in the early afternoon – a breathtaking rainbow forms above the plunge pool of this waterfall. Bathing in the fall's pool is also highly popular with local youths. The ascent to the viewpoint by the fall and the continuing hike on the left-hand side of the stream is possible also for children. But please be aware that descending into the plunge pool is pretty slippery and not without its risks.

→ **Directions:**
For directions, see spot 94. Parking spaces can be found next to the bus stop at Maggia, Centro.

→ **GPS:** 46.25048, 8.70617

SALINE SPA –
Maggia, Ponte Brolla

The river Maggia is inviting, with many beautiful bathing spots from its source at the Basodino glacier, at an altitude of 3,300m, down to where it flows into Lake Lago Maggiore. Arguably the most impressive spot is below the distinctive Ponte Brolla bridge at the turning into the Melezza valley. Inviting sandy beaches, which are also better suited for children, are to be found upstream at Avegno. There are flat gravel beaches by the suspension cable bridge at Aurigeno, and a big beach with catering facilities in the main village of Maggia.

→ **Directions:**
You get to the Maggia valley by car via the A13 to Locarno. Then follow the main road into the Val-lemaggia. Ponte Brolla is only 5km from Locarno. The other upstream locations listed here can be reached in successive order in only a few minutes by car. In peak season, it is recommended to take the bus from Locarno.

→ **GPS:** 46.18598, 8.75092

MILLS BY THE RUSHING STREAM –
Verzasca, Lavertezzo

It may not be everybody's cup of tea to jump 220m into the deep off the Verzasca reservoir dam, on a bungee rope, like a James Bond. You may indeed feel more at ease in the river's fabulously green natural pools. This spot is so incredibly popular that we almost feel inclined to discourage you from visiting it in high summer, except at the beginning or end of the day. Blessed are those who are able to enjoy this wild-swimming paradise in early or late summer when it is less crowded. The best-known bathing spot is by the Roman bridge in Lavertezzo, and there is another one directly in Brione.

→ **Directions:**
Travel into the narrow Verzasca valley via the A13, exit it at Locarno and follow the signs, which can't possibly be overlooked. There are 33 parking spaces by the river, and you will need to buy a Verzasca Parking Card (for CHF 10.00 per day). In peak season, however, it is strongly advised that you take the Post Bus from Locarno. For further information, visit www.postauto.ch/de/fahrplan.

→ **GPS:** 46.26003, 8.83614

96

TAMBO GROUP

A PURE SOURCE OF ENERGY –
Maglio del Malcantone, Ponte di Vello, Miglieglia

The chestnut region of Malcantone is attractive because it offers relatively big differences in altitude in a small area. Windy roads and interesting mountain-bike and hiking trails traverse the hilly landscape and dense forests, leading into the mountainous hinterland. The track to the Maglio hammer mill starts at the Ponte di Vello bridge and leads through open forest, always following the course of the river. In approx. 20 minutes you reach the small waterfall, including bathing pool, by the restored hammer mill.

→ **Directions:**
Exit the A2 at Lugano North and follow the signs to Malcantone on an ascending and bendy road for 10km, then take a right turning to Ponte di Vello/Breno.

→ **GPS:** 46.02480, 8.86849

97
SCHWYZ ALPS

Reuss Delta/Lake Lucerne, Flüelen

This nature reserve is located at the southern end of Lake Urnersee (Lake of Uri), which is a part of Lake Lucerne (Vierwaldstättersee). The region is characterised by reed meadows, low-moor marshes and alluvial forest and is a refuge for rare plants and amphibians. Close to the shallow shores are three islands, all of which are protected. The other islands, on the other hand, can be used as bathing spots. These islands were created using rock that was excavated when the Gotthard Base Tunnel was built. Several fire pits, changing rooms, loos and a kiosk make the Reuss delta a great spot for families too.

→ **Directions:**
  Exit the A2 at Flüelen or Seedorf and park at the Flüelen railway station or in the direction of Seedorf/Attinghausen in the car parks by the Forstgarten and Seerestaurant.

→ **GPS:** 46.89477, 8.60769

BATHING FUN IN A FORMER PRINCIPALITY –
Lake Lauerz, Lauerz

The Pleasure Island of Schwanau, including a restaurant, is located a few hundred metres from the southern shore of Lake Lauerz (Lauerzersee). You get to the island on the Gemma von Arth ferry. A more adventurous option for travelling is to swim across with your own swim buoy (see the image on the right), which also keeps your clothes dry. In this way, swimming fun and a visit to the restaurant can be combined in a dignified manner. If you are not so keen on the island, you can find further wild bathing spots and car parks on the mainland by the southern lakeside road. There is a public bathing facility in Seewen on the eastern shore.

→ **Directions:**
Exit the A4 at Seewen and follow Route Kantonstraße 2, direction Lauerz.
www.schwanau.ch

→ **GPS:** 47.03117, 8.59549

FAMILY SPOT WITH A MILL –
Lake Ägeri

The 7.3km-long Lake Ägeri (Ägerisee) was formed during the last glacial period due to the erosion of the Muota/Reuss glacier. Its water quality is excellent and since 1992 the lake has also been used as a reservoir. Lake Ägeri offers not just pleasure boat rides but also a wide range of options for hikers, cyclists and those who enjoy water sports. The most beautiful wild bathing spots are to be found on the lake's western and eastern shores, not very far from the lakeside roads, or in the centre of Ober-Ägeri in the former beach bathing section. The *"Lido"* in Unter-Ägeri is listed as the "official" public bathing section, and has all of the necessary facilities.

→ **Directions:**
Approach on the A4 and exit at Baar/Ägeri.

→ **GPS:** 47.10985, 8.62476

TWO UNIQUE, SPRING-FED POOLS –

Klöntalersee, Näfels

Originally, Lake Klöntalersee, at an altitude of 848m, was created as the result of a rock slide. In 1908, it was additionally dammed by a low wall and has since been used for hydropower generation. The lake has good water quality and warms to 22°C in high summer. The prettiest bathing spots are by the 7km-long hiking trail along the southern shore. While the trail is easy to walk, it is not suitable for pushchairs and wheelchairs. The Swiss poet Carl Spitteler, who was awarded the Nobel Prize for Literature in 1919, was enthused by views of the unique "fjord landscape", and wrote: "Those who have seen its solitude just once, at the right light, will not be able to forget this image for the rest of their lives."

→ **Directions:**
Exit the A3 at Niederurnen/Glarus and follow the signs to Näfels, Netstal, Riedern, Klöntalerstraße to the chargeable car park at Camping Güntlenau.

→ **GPS:** 47.03100, 9.00104

The "Obersee" (upper lake) is situated in a beautiful valley basin at an altitude of 983m. The pushchair-friendly hiking trail allows you to walk around the lake in an hour and to explore the various bathing spots along the way, as well as to watch people fishing. Afterwards, we recommend that you get something to eat in the "Berghotel" (mountain hotel), with its majestic viewing terrace and large selection of food and drinks. In parts, the shores of Lake Obersee can be very muddy. However, unadulterated bathing fun is to be had 1km behind the lake in the natural swimming pool, which is fed by a wild stream. Here, you will also find changing rooms, showers and a barbecue area.

→ **Directions:**
Exit the A3 at Niederurnen/Glarus and follow the signs to Näfels. From there, an approx. 4km long, well-signposted mountain road leads to the lake.

→ **GPS:** 47.08733, 9.01999

102

GLARUS ALPS

THE DEEP BLUE
Talalpsee, Filzbach

The wild landscape of the Glarus Alps is home to this idyllic mountain lake at an altitude of 1,084m. There are well-kept barbecue sites for self-catering all around Lake Talalpsee. During the summer months, the lovely restaurant, with its marvellous panoramic views, is also very inviting. During the warm months of the year, some hikers use the lake as a welcome option for cooling off, especially if they chose to take the 2-hour ascent from Lake Walen.

→ **Directions:**
For directions to Filzbach, see spot 103. It is possible to take the chairlift from Filzbach to Habergschwänd. From there, it is half an hour on foot to the lake. There is an option to make the return journey with a special scooter called a "*trottinet*". You can also drive to the lake on a toll road from Filzbach.

→ **GPS:** 47.09589, 9.13439

JUST ABOVE SEA LEVEL, AND ALSO BELOW IT –
Lake Walen

To many people, the Walensee (Lake Walen) is both the most beautiful and the cleanest lake in Switzerland. It would go beyond the scope of this guide to list all bathing spots that Lake Walen has to offer. One particularly charming "wild bathing spot" is on the "Pirate's Beach" in Tiefenwinkel. This is a small cove with a shady picnic site, sunbathing areas by the fine gravel beach and an excellent lakeside restaurant with a wonderful viewing terrace nearby. What more could you possibly want?

→ **Directions:**
Exit the A3 at Niederurnen/Glarus and drive to Näfels, and then follow Route Kerenzerbergstraße to Filzbach (102). From there, follow the road to Tiefenwinkel on Lake Walen. Here, follow the signs to Seerestaurant zur Brauerei. Park before the railway underpass or speak to the friendly restaurant owner to find another parking solution.

→ **GPS:** 47.11614, 9.18601

TRUE TO ITS NAME –
Gänglesee,
Triesenberg in Liechtenstein

Lake Gänglesee, which is fed by the Valünerbach stream, is actually a mud collection lake for the Steeg reservoir. However, it is regarded as the "only" mountain lake in Liechtenstein and is popular with bathers in summer. There are well-kept barbecue and picnic areas along its shores, as well as a rustic inn upstream of the bridge across the Valünerbach. From here, you can enjoy beautiful hikes into the alpine meadows of Liechtenstein.

→ **Directions:**
   Exit the motorway at Vaduz and drive in the direction of Triesenberg. Continue to Malbun. The journey should take you about 20 minutes.

→ **GPS:** 47.10629, 9.57781

(118) Arzino, Cerdevol

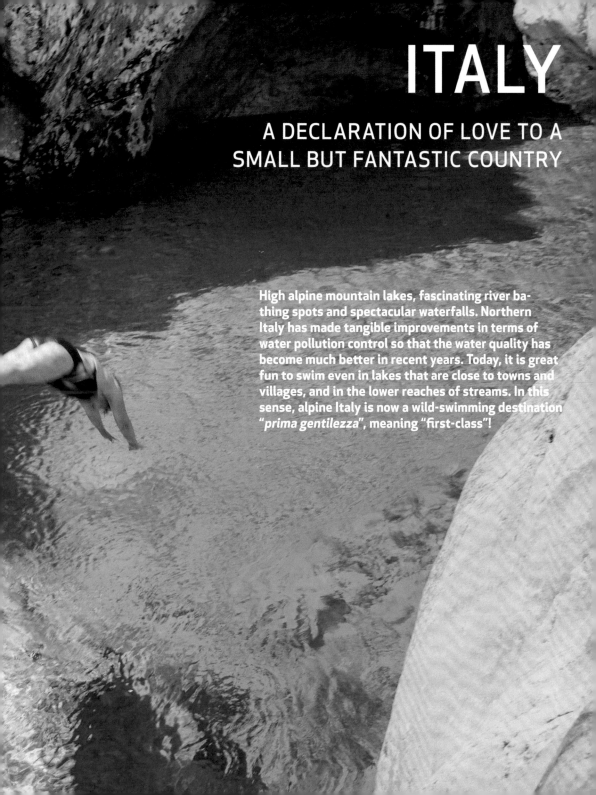

ITALY

A DECLARATION OF LOVE TO A SMALL BUT FANTASTIC COUNTRY

High alpine mountain lakes, fascinating river bathing spots and spectacular waterfalls. Northern Italy has made tangible improvements in terms of water pollution control so that the water quality has become much better in recent years. Today, it is great fun to swim even in lakes that are close to towns and villages, and in the lower reaches of streams. In this sense, alpine Italy is now a wild-swimming destination *"prima gentilezza"*, meaning "first-class"!

105

EXTREMELY EXTRAVAGANT –
Bergsee, Burgeis

The hamlet of Burgeis in the Upper Vinschgau is characterised by houses nestling close to each other, narrow alleyways, the imposing monastery of Marienberg, and Fürstenburg castle. In addition, there is the small Lake Bergsee, a mountain lake on a slope behind the hamlet with a fantastic view of the Ortler Alps. Hiking trail no. 3 takes you from the northern edge of Burgeis to the lake in half an hour. This hike, as well as the "*pausa*", a resting place by the 1,370m Bergsee, with a table, bench and fountain, inviting hikers to take a break, is highly recommended for families too.

→ **Directions:**
You get to Burgeis and Lake Reschensee close to the north (106) via the Reschenbundesstraße route, either approaching from the north via Landeck and the Reschen Pass or from the south via Merano. Park the car either in the village or near the sports ground.

→ **GPS:** 46.71577, 10.52703

106

ÖTZTAL ALPS

THE ROAD, THROUGH VINEYARDS, TO HEAVEN –

Reschensee, Graun

Today's Lake Reschen is relatively new. It was only created in 1950 by damming the river and combining three old lakes at the Reschen Pass. The village of Graun and a large part of the village of Reschen were submerged by the waters of the lake when a total of 163 houses and more than 500 hectares of land were flooded. Today, the church spire of the sunk village of Alt-Graun still stands tall above the water. You can visit the spire up until late summer by entering the church at ground level. Only in the autumn – when the reservoir is filling – does it become possible to swim to the church. The water temperatures are chilly, even in high summer when there are countless options for water sports along the shores of the lake. Due to its exposed location, Lake Reschen is an eldorado for kitesurfers.

→ **Directions:**
For directions, see spot 105. There is a chargeable car park by the church-spire viewpoint directly on the main road – the Reschenbundesstraße.

→ **GPS:** 46.81056, 10.53724

ESCAPE TO THE ISLAND –
Lake Molveno, Molveno

Lake Molveno, by the village of the same name, was formed after the last ice age as a result of a mighty rock slide. Today, the 4.4km-long lake, which is up to 124m deep, is used for hydropower generation. From its eastern shore, you have a wonderful view of the Brenta Group and the idyllic village of Molveno below. You can find many bathing spots here, some of which have facilities and all kinds of infrastructure, while others are unspoilt and "wild". The western shore, on the other hand, which can only be accessed via an old, steep cart track, is much more remote, and also rather difficult to access.

→ **Directions:**
Exit the A22 at Mezzocorona and take a right turning onto Route SS43 to Mezzolombardo. At the first crossroad, turn left to Fai della Paganella and follow Route SP64 to Andalo. There, follow Route SS421 to Molveno. Otherwise, exit the motorway at Trento North and take the highway into the Nons valley. From Riva del Garda, follow Route SS421 via Ponte Arche to Molveno.

→ **GPS:** 46.13824, 10.97018

INDEFINITE SWIMMING IN THE SALTWATER LAKE –
Lake Tovel, Tuenno

This gem of the Adamello Brenta Nature Park is at an altitude of 1,180m and has an almost triangular shape and crystal-clear water. The lake is surrounded by an enchanting mix of forest and high alpine mountains. The Lago di Tovel is sometimes called "Lago Rosso" (red lake). This is due to a phenomenon that occurred up until 1964, where algae blooming in the lake gave the water a blood-red colouring. The inn close to the car park is aptly called "Albergo Lago Rosso". A circular walk around the lake, taking approx. 90 minutes, leads you to magnificent natural bathing spots. These are located by the shore that is closest to the car park and rather hidden away in the woods. There are other spots on the opposite shore, and also on fine gravel stretches of shoreline.

→ **Directions:**
The Tovel valley is accessed via Route SP73 from Cles to Tuenno. From there, follow Route SP14 and the signs for the approx. 17km journey to the lake.

→ **GPS:** 46.26289, 10.95212

When the Santa Giustina reservoir was completed in 1951, its 153m-tall dam was the highest in Europe. The reservoir holds 185 million cubic metres of Noce water, which is not just used to generate electricity but also for all kinds of water-sport activities. Above the reservoir area is the river Noce, a wild mountain river that is ideal for kayaking and more extreme wild swimmers. Within the reservoir area, you can bathe by the Santa Giustina bridge (a) and further downstream by the village of Banco at the Bar Chalet al Lago. Swimming is also possible at Romallo in the Parco Fluviale Novella, in the canyons (b) formed by the wild stream of the same name.

→ **Directions:**
Approach from Bolzano via Route SS42 to the upper river Noce and the Santa Giustina bridge (turning onto Route SP139 at Cagno), or to Banco (turning onto Route A74 at Revo). www.mezzacorona.it

→ **GPS:** a), b) 46.38944, 11.03709

a)

LEGENDARY LOVE NEST –
Waterfall of Vilpiano, Terlano

This natural monument is fed by the Mölten stream, which, downstream of the fall, was used to irrigate the fields in the Vilpiano watercourse from as early as the 17th century. Later on, this was the site of a brewery that used steam to produce beer and was powered by a Pelton turbine. The turbine building has recently been restored and can be visited free of charge.

Today, the Tirolean firefighting academy occupies the former brewery premises, and it is here that you can park the car. The easy hike to the waterfall from the centre of the village takes 10 minutes.

→ **Directions:**
Terlano is situated on Route SS38 between Merano and Bolzano

→ **GPS:** 46.55907, 11.22886

111

PRAGS
DOLOMITES

COLLECTING MUSHROOMS IS PROHIBITED! –
Lake Prags

The mighty Seekofel mountain once had a slide of mud and debris, and this created a natural reservoir. Today, Lago di Braies (Lake Prags, or "Pragser Wildsee" in German) is arguably the most popular mountain lake in Italy. This reputation has been significantly helped by the much-loved Italian TV series *Un passo dal cielo* (meaning "very close to the sky"). The series was filmed in this location and you can still visit its set in the nearby "Seehotel" (lake hotel). Those who are looking for solitude at the "movie-like" mountain lake will need to get away from the hustle and bustle and walk the flat circular hike around the lake. They will be rewarded with fabulous bathing spots, crystal-clear and very cold water, and a marvellous panoramic view of the surrounding mountains. *Bene!*

→ **Directions:**
In principle, you can travel here by car via the Pustertaler Staatsstraße (Route SS49), direction Innichen – Niederdorf – Prags (SP47), and this will get you to the lakeside car park. However, please note that, due to overcrowding during peak season, from mid-June to mid-September, the road from Schmieden to Lake Prags is blocked between 10.30am and 2.00pm. In this case, you will need to walk from the chargeable overflow car park at Schmieden on trail 1, which gets you to the lake in approx. 1.5 hours. Otherwise, you can take the regular bus No.442i to the lake.

→ **GPS:** 46.69980, 12.08792

This bathing lake is surrounded by one of the few remaining wetlands in the Alps between the nature reserves of Tre Cime and Fanes Sennes Prags. The northern shore of the lake has well-kept bathing spots with facilities. It is possible to walk around the lake on a pretty nature trail that also leads you to more remote places and small coves. Please observe the signposted protected areas! Breathtaking Lake Toblach (Lago di Dobbiaco) is very popular with botanists, fishers and ornithologists due to its large number of rare species.

→ **Directions:**
Coming from the north via Toblach (Dobbiaco), follow the road through the Höhlenstein valley. If you are approaching from the south via Cortina d'Ampezzo, follow the road from Schluderbach (Carbonin).

→ **GPS:** 46.70479, 12.21958

GOLDEN BEACH ON A GREEN ISLAND –
Dürrensee

The Dürrensee (Lago di Landro) is in a picturesque location in front of the Cristallo Group,
only a few kilometres into the valley from Lake
Toblach. It is fed by wild streams from the nearby high mountains, the water tables of which
vary greatly throughout the year. As a result,
the lake's water level also varies depending on
the season. It is because of the lake's shallow
depth that it is warmer than comparable lakes
at this altitude. You can find beautiful bathing
spots on the southern and western shores. The
northern shore is very shallow and suited more
for children than for actual swimming. Hiking
trail no. 6a leads to a rock climbing area at the
foot of the rock face.

→ **Directions:**
For directions, see spot 112. Park by the restaurant slightly north of Lake Dürrensee or
directly in the car park on the main road.

→ **GPS:** 46.63291, 12.23216

This unspoilt reservoir is predominantly known for its incredible play of colours that, depending on the light, range from bluish to greenish tones. These colours are created by dissolved sediments that also give the water a very pleasant soft quality. This popular bathing lake is in the centre of a unique mountain landscape and is not only suitable for swimming but also for windsurfing, sailing, canoeing, kayaking and scuba diving. The surrounding area also offers ideal conditions for mountain biking, hiking and climbing. It is possible to bathe anywhere around the lake, and bathing is particularly easy directly in the centre of the village, not far from a small harbour.

→ **Directions:**
   Exit the A23 at Osoppo and drive via Forgaria nel Friuli, Sequals and Majont to Barcis. This journey is approx. 60km.

→ **GPS:** 46.18994, 12.56374

SIMPLY BEAUTIFUL –
Meduna, Navarons

The Tramontina valley is a real gem for lovers of wild swimming. Already along the lower reaches of the river Meduna there are many suitable sites. The wide bathing spot below the bridge is not just popular and easy to access but also ideally suited for families. Parking is possible on the road on both sides of the bridge, and it is best to descend towards a sandbank on the right-hand bank.

→ **Directions:**
Exit the A23 at Osoppo and follow the road via Forgaria nel Friuli, Travesio and Meduna for approx. 35km, until you get to the turning to Navarons.

→ **GPS:** 46.22483, 12.76008

ONE OF SHORTEST RIVERS IN EUROPE? –
Pozze Smeraldine, Tramonti di Sopra

The emerald ponds in the Friulian Dolomites Nature Park are no longer an insider's secret, and certainly haven't been since the British broadsheet *The Guardian* included them among the top 10 most beautiful villages, rivers and lakes of Italy. You can get to the ponds via an uncomplicated hiking trail that leads past the highly recommended Agriturismo Borgo Titol. This inn is great as a base camp or just for the tasty food it has to offer.

Wild bathing is also possible a few kilometres south in Tramonti di Sotto, by the Lago di Redona reservoir – ideally at its upper end where it is joined by the river Meduna.

→ **Directions:**
Exit the A23 at Tolmezzo and follow Route SS52 into the Tagliamento valley. In Priuso, turn left onto Route SR552 and drive via the spectacular Passo Rest pass on a windy road into the Tramontina valley.

→ **GPS:** 46.30990, 12.76379

117 a b | WHAT A STUNNING SETTING! –
Chiarsò, Campone

Campone is located slightly above the Tramontina valley on a very lovely upland plateau. If you
park near the picnic area (a) by the river, you can
take a quick dip by a small weir. Only a 10-minute
walk upstream is a 17th-century mill (b) where it
is also possible to bathe. From there, a 1.5-hour
hike, which leads along the river Chiarsò and
offers beautiful bathing spots, gets you to the
15m-tall Pisulat waterfall.

→ **Directions:**
  Roughly halfway between spots 115 and 116, directly by Lago di Redona, drive Route SP57 uphill
  and then take the turning to picturesque Campone.

→ **GPS:** a), b) 46.25922, 12.83364

a)

LIVELY ISLAND WITH A "DEAD SEA" –
Arzino, Cerdevol

The impressive Arzino valley features the Cerdevol Curnila, one of the arguably most beautiful sites for wild bathing in Europe. The valley is situated between Pielungo and San Francesco. Here, the white and red rocks, emerald water and deep pools, which are also suited for cliff-diving, will enchant anybody with a love for nature.

→ **Directions:**
If you are coming from the north (Tolmezzo), follow Route SP1 to the junction to Pielungo, keep right and, after 200m, park in the Curnila car park. Alternatively, when approaching from Campone (117), follow Route SP57 to Clauzetto and from there Route SP55 to Pielungo.

→ **GPS:** 46.28003, 12.93759

118) Arzino, Cerdevol (previous page)

Lake Cavazzo,
Cavazzo Carnico

We are looking at a giant. The biggest natural lake in the region of Friuli-Venezia Giulia has a length of 2.25km and a maximum width of 800m. In ancient times, a side arm of the river Tagliamento flowed through the Cavazzo valley, but today the reservoir at Verzegnis feeds the lake with very cold, deep water (approx. 10°C). In Bordano, on the eastern shore, is a butter-fly house and trail. The reed-bed area in the south is a spawning site for the lake's wealth of fish species as well as a retreat for numerous species of waterfowl. If you want to enjoy a quick swim en route, go to the bathing site in the far north where Regional Route 512 first runs parallel to the eastern shore. More facilities, including pedal-boat hire and a restaurant, can be found by the bathing area by Bar al Molo on the eastern shore, by the southern draining point of the lake.

→ **Directions:**
Approaching from the north, exit the Alps–Adriatic Sea motorway at Carnia-Tolmezzo. After the Tagliamento bridge, turn right, direction Cavazzo Carnico, and follow the si-gns to the campsites. If you are coming from the south, exit the motorway at Gemona/Osoppo-Trasaghis-Alesso-Lago di Cavazzo.

→ **GPS:** 46.34038, 13.07527

ALMOST IN MONTENEGRO –
Gailitz gorge, Tarvis

This climbing trail was created as early as 1874. It starts by the war memorial and leads onto a steep but well-secured path down through the forest and to the bank of the river Gailitz ("Slizza" in Italian). Once at the bottom of the gorge, the first pool – a small basin – invites you to have a refreshing swim. Then walk upstream past further marvellous bathing spots until you get to the old railway bridge. Here the trail leads uphill to a viewing point from which you can admire an 18m-tall waterfall. You can return to the car park in a few minutes via the Alps–Adriatic Sea cycling route.

→ **Directions:**
Follow the Alps–Adriatic Sea motorway to Tarvis and exit at Tarvis Boscoverde. Then turn left twice, direction Fusine. Approx. 150m after the motorway slip road to Villach, take a left turning to the car park at the Tarvis-Boscoverde railway station.

→ **GPS:** 46.50911, 13.60388

A SOURCE OF NATIONAL PRIDE –

Weissenfels Lakes, Valromana

JULIAN ALPS

The upper of the two Weißenfels lakes (Laghi di Fusine) is not just shallower and therefore warmer than its little sister but also more picturesque and remote in its beautiful setting below the mighty Mangart peak. The moraine wall, which separates both lakes, features many boulders that were transported here by the glacier aeons ago. One of these boulders, "Rudolf rock", has a volume of 30,000m³, making it the biggest glacial boulder in the southern Alps.

→ **Directions:**
For directions, see spot 120. Follow Route SS54 to Fusine. From there, take a right turning onto Via Lago and drive past the lower lake to the caravan park on the eastern shore. You can walk to the lake in a few minutes.

→ **GPS:** 46.47526, 13.66931

b)

a)

From Tarvis you can cross the Predil Pass to get to the picturesque Soca valley in Slovenia. Just below the top of the pass, and still on Italian soil, is Lake Raibl (Lago del Predil), known for its intense blue and green colours as well as its panoramic mountain views. There is a car park at its northern tip and nearby you will find a bathing spot by the small island. There is also a rustic restaurant by the name of "Chalet Al Lago". If you follow the lakeside road towards the south, roughly halfway down the lake, you get to a former bunker system and a car park. Here is a good spot to access the water and there is also a beach kiosk, surfboard and boat hire and an old gun that points out over the lake. At the southern tip of the lake, to your bottom-left in the wood, is a car park and a campsite (chargeable from 15 June to 31 August). The sediment delta, where the lake is fed by a mountain stream, and the area to the east feature beautiful and remote bathing spots with gravel and sandy beaches.

→ **Directions:**
Exit the Alps–Adriatic Sea motorway at Tarvis and follow the signs to Slovenia and the Predil Pass. If you are coming from the south, drive via Bovec through the Soca and Koritnica valleys.

→ **GPS:** a) 46.42709, 13.56796, b) 46.41555, 13.55809

b)

(125) Nadiža, Kobarid

SLOVENIA

A DECLARATION OF LOVE TO A SMALL BUT FANTASTIC COUNTRY

Close to the sky, the alpine part of Slovenia is formed by the Julian Alps, the Kamnik Alps/Karawanks and the Pohorje mountains. The 2,864m-tall Mount Triglav in the national park of the same name is the highest mountain in Slovenia. Its upland plateau is home to many breathtakingly beautiful lakes where swimming is sadly not permitted, to protect the environment. Irrespective of the above, Slovenia features countless rivers, lakes and waterfalls from the regions bordering Austria and Slovenia right into the karst areas.

The village of Bovec, which is a hot spot for sportspeople, is located at the confluence of the rivers Soca and Koritnica. Both of these are wild rivers much loved by kayakers, fly fishers and wild swimmers. However, please be aware that these rivers are very cold, even in summer, and without a warming neoprene suit only hardy swimmers should attempt to bathe in them. The green natural pool below the Virje waterfall is much more pleasant to swim in. The fall is located in the mountain village of Plužna, above Bovec.

→ **Directions:**
When you arrive in Bovec, follow the road towards the hydropower station and park the car before the bridge over the Glijun stream. From there, follow the signs to your left that lead you downhill to the waterfall. Coming from the north, exit the A23 at Tarvis and drive over the Predil Pass into the upper Soca valley (Bovec/1). For the middle section of the Soca valley (Kobarid 2,3), exit the A23 at Udine/Cividale del Friuli. To access the lower Soca valley (Tolmin/4), exit the A34 at Gorizia.

→ **GPS:** 46.33511, 13.51420

b)

b)

Soca, Kozjak waterfall, Kobarid

Here, the Soca valley opens up and Italy is just around the corner. Wild-swimming enthusiasts have a choice between the charming beauty of the Nadiža (125), the cool Soca (124a) and the wild Kozjak waterfall (124b). The hike begins at Napoleon's Bridge and can be done as a direct route, which is also less steep, from the Soca valley. Otherwise, there is an option to take a windy trail through old bunkers and fortifications from World War I and over a mountain ridge to the waterfall. The track then leads via a well-crafted path through a small gorge into a dark cauldron that is only lit from above. On top of that, you are also being showered with water from above. It is worth mentioning that the area of Kobarid is known for its excellent cuisine.

→ **Directions:**
For directions, see spot 123.
www.hisafranko.com.

→ **GPS:** a), b) 46.26261, 13.59405

A SOURCE OF NATIONAL PRIDE –
Nadiža, Kobarid

125

JULIAN ALPS

Local legend has it that this small but significantly warmer sister of the river Soca has healing properties. The river Nadiža's banks are lined by mighty willow trees that give it a particular charm. The best bathing spots are to be found around Podbela. The first spot is located to the east of the hamlet and, due to its shallow banks and easy-to-monitor location, is ideal for families with small children. There are also chargeable car parks here, as well as a picnic area and kiosk. A few kilometres upstream is Napoleon's Bridge, before the road begins a steep climb. Below the bridge, there is a magnificent natural pool.

→ **Directions:**
   In high summer, the bathing spots on the river Nadiža are overcrowded and the parking spaces rare and expensive. It is therefore recommended that you use the very reasonable hop-on-hop-off bus for €1.00 from the centre of Kobarid (see spot 123).

→ **GPS:** 46.22936, 13.43927

A SOURCE OF NATIONAL PRIDE –
Idrijca, Tolmin

126

JULIAN ALPS

The river Bača joins the river Idrijca by the village of Bača pri Modreju in the parish of Tolmin. You can experience wild swimming below imposing architecture here since the bathing spot on the river Idrijca is directly below a huge railway viaduct. It is easy to drive almost up to the river where you will find a large natural pool, a pretty beach and an improvised diving tower.

→ **Directions:**
For directions, see spot 123.

→ **GPS:** 46.14357, 13.76755

This rushing waterfall at the end of the Wo-cheiner valley is a popular tourist attraction. The main fall is off-limits for swimmers but there are some charming small basins and pools below the fall's mighty plunge pool. One of the most beautiful swimming spots of the "small Save" ("Savica"), which is easy to access and has a natural counter-current facility, is directly below the stone bridge at the entry point to the main fall.

→ **Directions:**
For directions, see spot 129. From there, drive along the river Save upstream for approx. 20 minutes until you get to the waterfall car park.

→ **GPS:** 46.29112, 13.79632

128) Lake Bohinj, Wochein (next page)

128

A SOURCE OF NATIONAL PRIDE –
Lake Bohinj, Wochein

JULIAN ALPS

The Wocheiner valley with the lake of the same name is right in the heart of the Julian Alps in the Triglav National Park – one of the oldest national parks in Europe. The biggest natural lake in Slovenia is surrounded by remote alpine meadows and mighty mountain peaks. Similarly to Lake Bled (Blejsko jezero), which is even more crowded, high summer brings large numbers of visitors to the lake. Hence, you will need a certain pioneering spirit or a boat to find a quiet spot. Best in this respect is the almost unspoilt northern shore. The tourist facilities, on the other hand, are predominantly located on the eastern shore. Easy-to-access bathing spots and chargeable car parks are to be found along the southern lakeside road.

→ **Directions:**
For directions, see spot 129. From Polje, drive into the valley for approx. 10 minutes until you get to the eastern shore.

→ **GPS:** 46.28150, 13.84707

Wocheiner Save, Polje

This emerald green wild stream is a paradise for kayakers, fishers and wild bathers, offering ample opportunity for swimming. Ideal for an uncomplicated bathing stop en route is the bathing area between Polje and Kamnje, with its own car park, Portaloo, picnic table and entry steps (this sounds less romantic than the spot actually is!).

→ **Directions:**
To get to the bathing spots in the Wocheiner valley, exit the A2 at Bled and drive for half an hour alongside Lake Bled on Route 209.

→ **GPS:** 46.26990, 13.91249

The legendary Mount Petzen is located on the border between Slovenia and Austria and is traversed by tunnels at various levels with a total length of an incredible 1,000km. One of the lower levels of the lead and zinc mine in Mežica, which was closed in 1994, was flooded a few years ago, and it is here where you can join a canoe tour (booking required and guided group tours only). Since 2019, I have been offering guided swimming tours in the tunnel's crystal-clear 9°C water. For more information, write to me at h.ransmayr@me.com.

→ **Directions:**
If you are approaching Mežica from Austria on the A2 from Klagenfurt, exit the motorway at Völkermarkt. Then follow Route B82/B81 to Bleiburg and the Slovenian Landesstraße 133 to Mežica.

→ **GPS:** 46.51110, 14.85587

OH BUOY
SWIM BUOY SAFETY

A HELMET FOR CYCLING,
A SWIM BUOY FOR WILD SWIMMING

The swim buoy is now mandatory at many open-water swimming events and is highly recommended to all responsible open-water swimmers.

Baywatch fans know about swim buoys as Pamela Anderson and David Hasselhoff used them to courageously dive into the ocean. Swim buoys have improved a lot since then. In essence, there are currently two different systems available. One of them combines the benefits of a safety device with those of a dry bag. In the following, we explain how the Swim 360 system works.

VISIBILITY

It is an eye-catcher. In open water, the predominantly high-visibility coloured buoys ensure that you are easily spotted. This is particularly important in areas where shipping traffic is to be expected. A freestyle swimmer, for example, has a very restricted field of vision, and they are also difficult to see in the water. Even if swimmers are visually tracked and monitored by observers, this is all much easier when colourful buoys are used. Even at night, the watertight battery-powered LED ribbons produce a glow effect that guarantees good visibility. Buoys are a must-have for all swimmers!

BUOYANCY

These swim buoys have an integrated air chamber that provides sufficient buoyancy to keep a swimmer afloat by holding on to them. Muscle cramping can happen easily on long swimming stretches or in cold water. In these instances, it is reassuring to have something you can cling to, resting until the cramping subsides.

A buoy also offers invaluable added safety in the event of other unpleasant surprises. It is not only children but also experienced pool swimmers who may suffer from unease or even panic attacks in unfamiliar open water. In the sea, such attacks can be provoked by jellyfish, for example, whereas in fresh water the touching of underwater obstacles such as seaweed or branches can be disconcerting to some. And sometimes, you might just want to give your body a little rest!

STORAGE SPACE

Apart from providing visibility and safety, swim buoys of this kind are also watertight bags for anything you want to take with you to the next shore. When rolled up, swim buoys are neat and small, but they offer you this attractive added function. This is because they have storage capacity above the air chamber. The proven roll-and-bend fastener ensures that the buoy is watertight. The size of a swim buoy depends on the model.

Handling these swim buoys is easy: 1. unroll, 2. store your things, 3. inflate the air chamber, 4. close the roll-and-bend system and fasten the waist belt. Done. In the water, the buoy is dragged behind you at a distance of approximately 1m so that it doesn't get in the way of your breaststroke or crawling. In fact, you won't notice the swim buoy at all, except in heavy swell or strong wind. Even when the buoy is fully loaded, it won't bother you.

Smaller swim buoys are often just big enough to store a mobile phone, car keys, a wallet and a T-shirt. The large and extra-large versions, on the other hand, offer significantly greater storage capacity of up to 30 litres. This means that nothing needs to be left behind on the shore. When swim-hiking or swim-running, after having crossed a lake, you can continue your tour on the opposite shore without having to return to the point where you started swimming. If you take your mobile, there are apps available for documenting the swimming route via GPS.

A scaled-down version or an "anachronistic" predecessor of this type of swim buoy is the Wickelfisch, a water-proof swim bag originally developed by Swiss Rhine swimmers and used to carry their stuff from one bridge on the river to another.

RESTUBE:
INFLATED IN SECONDS

If you feel that safety and compactness during open-water swimming are more important than additional storage space, the Restube buoy is your device of choice. This small bag with its waist belt hardly counts as added baggage. It contains the buoy and a CO_2 cartridge. In an emergency, you just pull the trigger. The buoy is filled with gas in seconds and provides enough buoyancy to comfortably rest on it. This is a principle known from the self-inflating life jackets on aeroplanes, or from alpine ABS avalanche backpacks.

The Restube is not just of interest to open-water swimmers but also to anyone else who cares about safety near and in the water, such as kayakers, windsurfers, sailors and outdoor enthusiasts in general. Most open-water swimmers carry the Restube in its already inflated state. While the Restube offers the benefits of improved visibility to others, as well as safety, it doesn't have any storage capacity. In heavy swell and strong wind, the relatively low drag of the buoy fixed to your waist can be an advantage. This also applies to swimming in groups, since the other swimmers can't get entangled in the buoy's belt. Whatever system you decide on, a swim buoy is a worthwhile investment for any activity that goes beyond wild dipping.

About the author

In his wild youth, Hansjörg was an enthusiastic alpinae kayaker. During those early years, he had already swum in the cold alpine waters, sometimes voluntarily and at other times less so, when the power of the whitewater proved stronger than him and his boat! It was only a small step from there to the open water. And it was the open-water swimming where the man from Salzburg earned his first stripes in salt water. He was the first Austrian to swim the Strait of Gibraltar, and he managed to cross the ice-cold water from the prison island of Alcatraz to San Francisco "by fair means". In 2010, he was the first and only Austrian to participate in the Winter Swimming World Championships in the freezing water of Lake Bled. Being a man of the mountains and a keen mountain hiker, it was only logical that Hansjörg soon discovered his love of native mountain lakes and wild water. He founded the Facebook group Wildswimming World and the info blog alpine-swimming.com. With these online activities, he also employs his many abilities honed during his decades-long career as Creative Director of an advertising agency. He has written several books on wild swimming and works as a free-lance concept developer, copywriter and author.

Hansjörg is also involved in various TV and film projects on topics around wild, alpine and ice swimming. Under the slogan "Swimsalabim", a play on a German word suggesting a magical instantaneous occurrence, he creates events and swimming projects for tourist associations. He also consults mountain cableway/railway operators concerning the utilisation of water collection ponds for snow cannons during the summer months. In addition, he offers guided tours and travel in the sector of swim hiking, swim adventure and swim enjoyment. As a certified mountain hiking guide and active lifeguard, he is particularly interested in the topic of safety by and in the water. This is one of the reasons why Hansjörg is heavily involved in the development of innovative products, such as the SWACK, for use in open-water swimming. Furthermore, he is a core member of both the Austrian and international open-water and ice-swimming community.

Hansjörg Ransmayr

(1) Stuibenfälle, Reutte

SWIM WILD

Wild Swimming
Alps

130 most beautiful lakes,
rivers & waterfalls in Austria,
Germany, Switzerland, Italy
and Slovenia.

Text & photos by
Hansjörg Ransmayr

Edited by
Katharina Theml, Büro Z,
Wiesbaden, Germany

Translated by
Thomas Moser

Designed by
Margaret Prepasser

Typeset & proofread by
Patrick Davies

First published in German by
Haffmans Tolkemitt, 2019

This edition published by
Wild Things Publishing Ltd.
Freshford, Bath, BA2 7WG

Distributed by
Central Books Ltd
50, Freshwater Road
Dagenham, RM8 1RX
020 8525 8800
orders@centralbooks.com

Contact:
hello@
wildthingspublishing.com

Health and safety and liability: Like all other activities on or by the water, swimming in nature carries risks and can be dangerous. This is explained in greater detail in the appendix. The locations described in this book are prone to both flooding and drought, as well as other changes. While the authors and the publisher have made every effort to ensure that the information is correct, they cannot assume any liability, neither legal nor financial, for accidents, injuries, loss of property or any other inconvenience that may result from the information or advice provided in this book. Swimming, jumping into the water, diving, scuba diving or any other activity in the locations described in this book are carried out exclusively at your own risk. If you have questions or are in doubt concerning any of the information provided in this book, please ask an independent party for advice.

Other books from Wild Things Publishing